AF427460

WHAT OTHERS SAY

"A very personal, vivid, and timely description of the dangers of an abusive relationship, and the courage it takes to break free from it."

— **Dr Goh Chee Leong**, CEO, HELP Education Services; Vice President; Dean, Faculty of Behavioural Science, HELP University; Past President, Malaysian Psychological Association (PSIMA)

"I can't say enough for how genuinely inspirational this whole book was. It's one I couldn't put down — and I would read it again."

— **Armaan Khadar**

"Trust Overboard takes us on a journey, one where love simply isn't enough. It's a true story of a young lady whose dreams of a happily-ever-after was violently torn away from her. Instead, she was thrown headfirst into a life of manipulation and spite, a life she neither understood nor deserved. It's a struggle to put the book down as Liya Red immerses her readers in the delivery of an unsettling story — one of abuse, suffering, and recovery."

— **Karthini M.**, avid reader and traveller

"Gripping and utterly compelling. Liya Red takes you inside the violent, devastating world of abusive love, where love and rage danced intimately together. Find out for yourself if she truly fell in love — or into a psychological trap. Trust Overboard will draw you in, and never let go."

— **Nereshpal G.**

"Liya Red brings us on a literary journey that captures a sense of excitement and anticipation as the pages unfurl. One minute excruciatingly painful, the next, joyful glee, she takes readers on a journey that compels one to read the whole book in a single sitting. There are books that can be read casually, over a few days or weeks. And then there's Trust Overboard, which requires an intense full day sit-down, for the anticipatory 'what now?' as every chapter comes to an end."

— **PK**, Founder and CEO, Tailor Made Writers

Trust Overboard: Memoir of Living with a Sadistic Cult in Malaysia

Copyright © 2017, 2018 by Liya Red

All Rights Reserved.

No part of this book may be reproduced or transmitted in any form or by any means, electronic or mechanical, including photocopying, recording, or by information storage and retrieval systems, without written permission from the author, except in the case of brief quotations in articles or reviews.

This is a work of nonfiction.

Some names and identifying details have been changed to protect privacy.

Published by Liya Red

For more information, visit: linktr.ee/liyared

Disclaimer:

This memoir reflects a past period in the author's life. While the events described are true, the author's perspectives and beliefs may have evolved since the time of writing.

Trust Overboard

Memoir of Living with a Sadistic Cult in Malaysia

LIYA RED

For the years I wasted away my love.

And most importantly, my trust.

CONTENTS

FOREWORD

Trust Overboard has certainly opened my eyes to another side of Malaysia that exists below the mainstream radar.

Liya Red's personal experience has frighteningly brought to light the horror and danger that domestic violence victims face.

Although her intention is to help Muslim women – this book is a good reminder for everyone to be on alert about manipulative behaviour, though mother-in-laws are on a totally different playing field.

WAO hopes that everyone reads this and together we will move forward to a better future.

Regards,
Carol Chin
President
Women's Aid Organisation
2017/9

PREFACE

I wasn't in touch with anyone in Malaysia when I was in Texas. After moving to Malaysia for good, I lived on my own and continued being in my comfort zone, with my third culture friends, or anyone who spoke English and were comfortable with the Western culture.

When I found Islam, I was happy that my college mate Adam knew a lot about it and he seemed to have higher morals than what I was used to with men in the Western culture. After being married, Adam became a completely different person. As all surprised wives of domestic abuse, I was shocked and confused when Adam started being abusive. It was difficult for me to believe it was really him. Concurrently, others around him appeared just as disturbed.

The story starts off with my meeting with a Syariah lawyer, to debrief on what I went through over the years. This narrative does not describe every abuse and offense I've endured. It rather focuses on the nature of the sadistic cult I wasn't aware I was in. I don't wish for sympathy, nor do I wish for over-emphasis on violence in this book. This book is not about Islamic spirituality. Private information, sex, intimacy, or anything unrelated to the story, whether positive or negative, have not been mentioned.

After freeing myself, I searched for the solution to heal. I continued making sense of the possible psychological disorders the cult might have. However, as I proceeded with the research, I realized I have since been doing so for the past few years. On the contrary, there's a much more important question. Why aren't people aware of it? I wrote this book for many reasons. One of them was in the hopes of increasing awareness of the cult that exists, and that is conceivably accepted. More specifically, amongst the Malays, and amongst the

Muslims, in Malaysia. I also wrote this book in the hopes of helping abused women everywhere overcome their doubts, and to cope. I hope they can gather some tips or inspiration from what I chose to do. I hope abused Muslim women, especially, can find hope in leaving their broken marriages.

This story could be helpful to study domestic abuse, cults, geopolitics, as well as psychological syndromes and disorders. Additionally, differences in the Muslim community, and of Malays in Malaysia, can be subject matters for analysis.

Liya Red, November 2018

DISCLAIMER: The stories in this book reflect the author's recollection of events. In writing this book, collection of phone conversations, emails, photos, and recordings, have been used for accuracy of occurrences. Some names have been changed to protect the privacy of individuals. Dialogue has been re-created from memory, though they are not written to represent word-for-word transcripts. Rather, the author has retold them in a way that evokes the feeling and meaning what of was said, and in all instances, the essence of the dialogue is accurate. The author is not responsible for any contents further discussed by readers or if any damage occurs by the use of information presented in this book.

ACKNOWLEDGMENTS

First and foremost, I thank God for everything He has willed and blessed me with. I couldn't have ever survived with this story, if it weren't for Him.

I thank my mom for having faith in me and allowing me to live independently. I'm stronger for that. I thank my older brother Ace for always defending me, and my younger brother Razz for taking time off to keep me safe.

I'm grateful to Nate for keeping me grounded, Tina for the emotional support, and Aaron, for reminding me of humanity. They helped me more than I thought I needed. I'm also grateful to Dee for always teaching me something new, and to Tasha, for her understanding.

Behind the scenes, I thank my Syariah lawyer for the generosity, and Sisters in Islam, for all the tips. I also thank the Sergeant for the security, and the policewoman for the female empowerment. I couldn't have gotten out positively without any of them.

Many thanks after the divorce to all who gave me their beautiful, supportive words, and well wishes. I couldn't have felt better without them. Moreover, I thank all those who came to see me at the wedding, and all those who came to see me on other days. Furthermore, I'm grateful to all those who have been understanding with me throughout the years. For being kind, patient, and forgiving, to any wrong that I may have caused.

Thank You
Liya Red

1

THE BEGINNING OF THE END

The meeting room was just enough to walk in. The lady at the front desk told me to wait there. I sat on one of the blue swivel chairs at the very end. Closest to the door, but not the first chair that's obviously for the boss. The table was big enough for ten people. On it a glass bowl of candies, small bottles of water, fake flowers placed together. In the top right corner of me, a CCTV. I adjusted myself. I imagined older people with twisted lives have been there.

The sound of the doorknob stopped my dreaming. A handsome head popped in to greet me. A tall, big, and lean middle-aged man. The lawyer I've been wanting to meet. The boss, the owner of the firm. I didn't expect him to look like that. I thought he'd be younger, average sized and at least nerdy looking. I was happy he's the one I got. He looked very smart, experienced, not easy to fool. Intimidating. Lucky for me he does Syariah law cases, too. Muslim women can't easily get a divorce if she's the one that wants it. It has to either be granted by the husband, or there has to be a very good reason with solid evidence for it.

No doubt a very busy man. He couldn't stop laughing to himself as he sat down, checking messages on his phone every few minutes while talking to me, excusing himself. I was the opposite. I felt like a goldfish in a bowl, unable to swim anywhere else. I watched him through my fishbowl.

"I would actually prefer your mom to be here, so that everything can be cleared up with everyone, and everything is understood," he told me, while stretching his arms out toward the empty chairs to show me.

"Oh… she wants her children to be independent. So I do everything myself," I said.

Ever since my mom lost her husband, I felt she lost a part of herself as my mother. She always made me worry about her by how much she worried about me. Then eventually, she started encouraging more independence, when she had enough of me stubbornly begging to learn from experience. She blessed me with independence at eighteen years old by giving me a gold key charm necklace with the number '21' on it, a necklace her mother gave her when she first got her freedom at twenty-one years old. I was a few years earlier and I was so proud to have it. That was also when I first moved out to live on my own. "You can go anywhere you want, you can do whatever you want -- as long as you don't ask anything from me, and you don't bother me with it," she said confidently with her right hand pointing in the air in front of her, while sitting on the right side of her floral king bed unmoved with her phone and throw pillows around her. It sounded like complete independence, a dream come true for a teenager, but not true. She still nagged all the time about my studies and my g-strings lying around in her bathroom -- her two favorite topics with me. I knew I still had to put up with everything because I was still financially dependent on her. Meaning, I was asking her for something and I couldn't even take a single semester break because of it. And my thongs in her bathroom still bothered her view when I left them there after using it. I always liked her bathroom more.

"Okay, I don't want to interfere with that. Good that she wants you to be independent," he paused to think. He continued to ask, "Umm… and your dad?"

"He passed away," I said.

He nodded at me and checked his phone for the last time.

"Okay, tell me," he said quickly, while looking at me, as he placed his phone further away from me and asked me for a pitch I wasn't ready for.

"I've been emotionally abused --"

"Emotionally?" he leaned forward to interrupt me like it was a joke.

"Well, physically," I answered, realizing what he meant was for why I was in trouble. "And, emotionally... and psychologically..." I added, like someone lowered the volume.

"Okay. Is that it?" he asked in a rush.

"He abused me to cover up, to speak Malay --"

"You don't speak Malay?"

"I do, but sometimes it's awkward. I wasn't raised here. My friends are foreigners. I went to an international school when I moved here," I said. I was shaking. I thought he wouldn't understand.

"Where were you raised?"

"Texas."

"For how long?"

"About ten years since seven," I said. Then I randomly blurted out, "And I'm still so young...!" as if he was supposed to grant me the divorce for being young.

Maybe he was holding in his laugh when he asked me, "How old are you?"

"Twenty-seven," I answered.

He paused to think about it and asked, "How long have you been married?"

"Three years."

"Okay, so you got married at... Twenty-four years old."

"Yes," I confirmed.

He nodded. "And your husband?"

"He's two years older than me."

"Let's see your marriage certificate," he said.

I quickly handed it to him from the folder I had prepared in front of me.

He looked at the first page and said, "Oh, he's American."

"Yeah."

"White?" he asked.

"He's half Malay, half British. His mom's Malay, and his dad's British. He was born in America, and raised in Malaysia," I told him. To be clear with the perception, I added, "His attitude, character, the way he speaks and everything... are all very Malay."

"What do you mean 'very Malay'?"

"He's just... so... Malay... Everything."

"I'm Malay," he said, pointing one hand to his chest quickly, and back to hold the certificate.

"I know, me too. I don't know how to explain it, he's just..."

"You mean his mentality," he said.

"Yeah... mentality..." I answered hesitantly, and slowly.

I never really liked saying that, because it makes me feel like I'm insulting my own race. But it's the truth anyway. The 'Malay mentality' are of the typical Malays that my cousin Dee warned me about. I remember it like it was just yesterday. How awkward I felt being at the small, overcrowded part of the airport in Malaysia we arrived at together. It was dark outside through the big glass windows. The fluorescent lighting inside seemed so blurry, dim, and foggy, odd-looking strangers staring, it almost felt unreal. Dee from London, and my mom, my two younger brothers and I, from Texas. My two older brothers continued living in Texas for a few more years, so they weren't there to laugh or communicate with me telepathically as we normally would by then. I wasn't used to my little brothers in situations like that. Especially not after all that we were going through. I met Dee like we never had silence between us, from when I was a little girl and she was a young adult. She warned me about many things in Malaysia. She had so much to say, her voice faded in my mind while I wondered what it would be like for me. I acted like I was listening most of the time. I was always good at that.

"My daughter's like you, too," he said. "She goes to an international school."

"Oh, I went to Mont'Kiara, what about your daughter?" I was relieved. There's a reason he can understand me, at least.

"Can't afford it," he paused to look at my reaction, and quickly showed he was joking. "Fairview."

Mont'Kiara was known to be the most expensive. I laughed, but only silently to myself. I was still a goldfish.

I opened my laptop to show photos of what Adam, the man I married, did to me over the years. I waited for his response like it was my resume.

"Yeah," he said with certainty while leaning back. His eyes locked on the screen, scrolling through. "You definitely couldn't have faked these photos. They look like something you can only see in CSI or something," he said, shaking his head.

I immediately felt sad. I felt so stupid. I had no answer.

"And he doesn't wanna let you go?" he asked.

"No," I answered. I felt anxious. I wasn't sure if I could ever get a divorce. I heard a lot of rumors about Syariah law being biased against women, always favoring men. Apparently they do this because many women would fake their way out of their marriage. Women tend to be more fickle, causing unnecessary problems.

"He loves you, he loves you not..." he said sarcastically, while going through more of the evidence.

"Exactly," I said.

He seemed uneasy from it and asked me, "Would he *ever* divorce you?"

"Not at all, never," I said, with absolute certainty.

"Where are you staying now?" he asked me, concerned.

"My mom's."

"Okay. What does he do? Your husband."

"He has a motorbike workshop in the city, at Jalan Ipoh," I quickly answered. It was Adam's current business, after the many businesses he had before.

"Is that his main income?"

"No, he gets some money from his mom sometimes," I said, while recalling having the groceries that his mom, Khatijah, would buy sometimes. Khatijah always liked us having her groceries more than our own. She got upset if we got anything that she already bought. Which is very understandable. But it wasn't always easy to take note of every single thing there was. Who goes to the grocery store for some eggs, and coming out with just eggs, anyway?

"What's her income like?" he asked me.

"She receives 12k ringgit per month pension from the IMF," I said, from what Adam told me. Some Islamic scholars told them that she should find herself some faith, stop it immediately, and repent, because the income contradicts the Islamic teachings of not supporting usury or something like that. But she never did, ironically, while focusing so much on *my* money.

"That's it?" he asked.

"Yes."

"Yeah, it seems like he doesn't know how risky it is for him. They can really lose a lot. He really won't divorce you?"

"No," I said, feeling sad. "I tried to get him to go through the mutual 'Fast Track' divorce, but on that day we were supposed to go, he suddenly changed his mind and told me 'go do it yourself' and ran out of the car. That's why I contacted you."

He was going through papers and taking notes.

"Does he know you have all the photos?" he asked.

"I don't know. I told him, but maybe he didn't believe me," I said. Or maybe he's like one of the Muslim boys who think they can treat their wives like shit, and that women have no way of leaving marriages, and that they're above women. But I didn't say that. I remained calm.

"Have you tried telling him what his risks are if he doesn't go through a mutual divorce...? First of all, it will be very ugly, and very messy. There will be a stand, where the public can watch, and all the evidence will be shown. It can take years, especially if he continues to be difficult... Police reports and medical reports must be submitted by you, and will forever be in his records. Bad for this case, and bad for his future... It's a *guarantee* especially if he does the same thing again to someone not as nice as you, someone who would fight back, even if it's a tiny pinch mark... If that happens, she immediately wins the case without going through it, because they can see the reports you once made as his wife. And, regardless of what happens in court, in the end, he will have to give you half of everything he owns, his car, his workshop, and anything he took care of while you were his wife, including money for all the days, weeks, to even years of allowance that you didn't receive during the entire divorce period. And also," he paused and looked up to think, "some extra amount that can be claimed, usually ranging from 50k to 100k," he told me.

I took note of it. Sounds good. I imagined calling all the media, societies and organizations to come support me with banners and everything, in court.

"But he's still a brother in faith. If he believes in God and the Prophet, he prays five times a day, he fasts during the holy month of Ramadan, you know, he's still a brother to us, so we must choose to deal with him in the nicest way," he said.

I remained quiet. I didn't want to tell him that all he's assuming wasn't true. Adam has cursed God and the Prophet, he wasn't praying five times a day, and I had never seen him fast during Ramadan properly, if he did at all. I wasn't used to talking bad about Adam, not even the slightest clue to anyone that he's been abusing me. I've only ever persevered in giving him positive reputation as my husband. The only time I ever could reveal anything, was when they were necessary for people to help me. I wasn't sure if it was necessary to reveal more then, because all I wanted was to leave the marriage. I didn't care about the money. I didn't even care about how difficult it would be or all that I would have to reveal in court. I just wanted it done as soon as possible, however possible soon was going to be.

"You must tell him the two options for divorce again. He's obviously not in a reasonable state of mind, so talk to someone else that he would listen to. Tell that person, so that he can tell your husband for you. Do you know anyone that you can talk to?"

"I guess either his uncle… or his cousin. I'll talk to his cousin, 'cause he's also his business partner," I answered.

He said to me slowly, "Okay, talk to his cousin. Just be genuine with him, and tell him you want to meet him to talk about something, because Adam is in an unreasonable state of mind. Show him how genuine you are that you would meet him for it."

"Should I contact his wife first?" I asked.

"No need," he shook his head. "You don't want any unnecessary emotions. He can tell his wife himself if he wants, and he can tell Adam and everyone in the family after. But no need to make things bigger. Keep things peaceful. Make copies of the photos before the meeting, in case anything happens… and don't go alone. Take your time… You're not rushing, right? You're not getting married anytime soon, right?"

"No, I never wanna get married anymore," I said with certainty.

"No, don't think like that," he closed his eyes and shook his head slightly, "Have faith that you'll find someone good for you in the future. Don't lose hope. Don't be scared. You're so fragile! I walked in and I already felt bad for you! You look so fragile. I don't want you to think everyone's bad. I'm worried you're seeing the world negatively now. Don't think like that. Be positive."

I sighed. He's right. I think. I still couldn't imagine being in a relationship anymore. How would I trust anyone else?

We packed up our things as he asked me some last questions.

"Are you working, do you need his support?" he asked.

"No, I have money," I said. We got up to leave the room.

"How?"

"I was modeling, before I got married. So I have a lot from that," I assured him.

2

THE AGREEMENT

When I first met Adam, we were attending the same private university. We met in the first year I was there. He was always in a serious relationship with one girl, throughout the years. I admired that, for someone to stay committed to another for so long, even though it didn't last in the end. Still, I always thought he would be a sweet and romantic guy because of that. I never believed he would be as romantic as my ex-boyfriend, though, who I was always too focused on to even care about Adam.

Adam drove a very old car, and he rode his big motorbike to uni sometimes. It was always when I thought he looked his best. He had a waist pouch that he always wore, and I liked that because my dad wore a waist pouch when he would be travelling or on his motorbike, too. It was the first thing I noticed about Adam when I first met him. It was always a positive thing for me to be reminded of my father, of course.

Usually, in the perspective of locals in Malaysia, Adam looked Caucasian. I always thought he didn't, though. He always made me think he's Malay, even when I saw him from a distance. I guess having Caucasian friends my entire life helped me distinguish his look. Adam was light skinned like me, and also similar to me, he was relatively tall compared to the average Malaysian. His hair was much darker than mine, that is dark brown. His was almost black, creating a very bold contrast to his face and emphasizing it. He had long healthy eyelashes that many girls were envious of. He had very thick eyebrows, too. Throughout the years, I've seen him chubby, and thin, then by the time he was courting me, he maintained a fit athletic body with muscles.

I spent a significant amount of time with him in uni to feel comfortable with him. We were always on good terms with our friendship, gradually growing over the years. He was fun, light hearted, and always joking with me. I was living on my own as a student, moving from one residence to another at least once a year, always welcoming anyone to hang out. I would meet him sometimes outside of uni, too, just as how I would meet anyone whenever they wanted to as well.

We especially started getting very close when we were taking the same subject and working on a group assignment together. Which, the meetings would normally be at my place. He had already broken up with his ex-girlfriend by then, so it was also our first time being single at the same time. I chose to be single ever since I got out of a relationship a year before. My ex-boyfriend, Romeo, was born Catholic. He was my best friend since high school who I ended up being in a relationship with for a few years during uni. I believe we were taken over by pride in the end. We couldn't decide how to go about an interfaith marriage. But it was never going to be easy anyway since he was back in his hometown, Holland. That was also what got me thinking more about Islam, the faith I was born with. I started my studying from there, whenever I had the time.

Adam and I fell for each other when he started coming over on his own, without our other group members. He opened up about his lifestyle, about living alone with his mom and taking care of her. I was so touched by it. What a good boy, I thought. He's also an only child and his father passed away when he was just three years old.

He told me about his relatives when he appeared to be annoyed, looking at his phone.

"What's wrong?" I asked him.

"My relatives are giving my mom a hard time in the group chat," he told me.

"Why are they doing that?" I asked.

"They always create problems with her. There's always drama," he said.

I never heard of something like that before, that a family would keep picking on a certain family member. It seemed to me like his family had some personal issues with his mom.

"Aww, then you should defend her. If they disrespect her, then you should tell them off," I told him, feeling sad for his mom, Khatijah. "You should always defend your mom, no matter what," I said to him. "If I were you, I would."

"Okay," he responded. He seemed positive again, and he continued to use his phone, typing. Then he said, "Okay, I told them off."

"What did you tell them?" I asked him.

"I told them to respect her more," he said.

It felt good that he valued my opinion to the point of making a difference in his family. I started trusting him more since then, because he allowed me into his personal life so much.

What really captured my attention, though, was how he responded to my interest in Islam. I was always spiritual, even when I was upset with God for years, for taking away my dad. I was exploring various faiths after his death, and I got to Islam again after my breakup with Romeo. I was researching on it when I had free time. Adam apparently knew a lot about it, and he seemed so interested in teaching me after I opened up to him about where I was spiritually. I never told anyone else. It seemed like perfect timing that I chose to open up to him and he had all the information for me in return.

He turned on some YouTube videos for us to watch together sometimes, to teach me about the bad condition of the world and its politics against Islam. I was surprised by all the things in the world I never realized was happening. He also taught me how to purify myself in the Islamic way, and how to pray and say the prayers correctly. I was impressed. I knew I didn't know anyone else that would be able to offer me this. He was satisfying my spiritual needs, my cravings of Islam. It was hard to deny the passion I had for it.

As we spent more time together, I learned that he cared about me more than I realized. Some, not all, of my college mates, were suddenly not asking me to hang out anymore when I was getting close to him. Maybe it seemed like we were dating. But some obviously just hated it. Perhaps they were too surprised, or perhaps even envious. It naturally got me even closer to him after welcoming him more and seeing him treat me best.

Adam emotionally supported me against people who were rude to me, and he offered to give rides back home without me asking him. He was very sweet and caring. He asked me to be his girlfriend, but I said 'No'. I never wanted a boyfriend again since Romeo. I've only been dating, but with no commitment. He respected it, and he immediately knew he would marry me. I was surprised by his spontaneity, but I felt I've known him for years as not only a college mate, but as one of my good friends. I always trusted him a lot, because he never gave me a reason not to.

The first and most crucial questions I had for him were, "What about my life? How would everything be? Can I still live my life the same way?"

And his answer was, "Yes, don't worry, everything's going to be the same."

I looked around my bedroom imagining myself married, but still, with independence. That's what I wanted. It made sense to how I would live my life. I've always been a social butterfly, and an independent workaholic at the same time.

Since I was sure about winging it with Adam while also still studying, I discussed with my mom to really make it happen. Adam and I planned to ask our moms because of this. My mom kept saying 'No' at first, till she decided to give it a shot and asked me some questions.

"He has no proper job and he's still studying. How are you ready?" my mom asked.

"According to Adam, we are, with his small businesses," I answered. Adam was mainly focusing on a burger stall he was running and managing at the time, with some other small businesses he had on hold on the side with his partners.

"Are you prepared to live with his mother?" she asked.

"Yes, I can take care of her for the rest of my life," I said. I knew Khatijah was a middle aged woman, but we were supposed to live with her for as long as we had to take care of her, just as Adam always has been. I was very open to living with her and doing so. It didn't matter how long it was going to be.

"Do you know that married couples need privacy?" she asked in another way, to be sure.

"I'm not bothered about that, because his mom would respect our marriage," I said, confidently. "It's his mom, anyway, and she's religious."

"You know there are many terrible mother-in-law stories, right?" she gave me an observant look for my answer.

"Yeah, well, she won't be like that... she's religious," I repeated myself, again, with confidence.

"Do you know his family well enough to be prepared to live with them for the rest of your life?"

"No, I don't. But I'll love them as my own," I assured her.

My mom felt more relaxed by that. She accepted Adam when he came to see her to ask for my hand in marriage. Before getting engaged to him, however, I was anxious about the marriage entirely. I didn't tell anyone about it. I didn't even feel any excitement of spreading the good news to anyone, at all. Not a single soul. I did some research on it and apparently it's just normal to be nervous. I wasn't sure what that 'normal' feeling should be like, but I was sure feeling nervous. I was filled with doubt.

I talked to my mom's older sister, Aunt Zee, one day when my mom invited me to visit her. Aunt Zee made me feel optimistic about it in the end.

She said, "Treat your mom-in-law well, so that if anything bad were to happen between you and Adam, his mom can help you better. Woman to woman."

I realized that's true. That as a woman, his mom would be there to support me. I felt better, thinking that I would still have support and advice from an older woman.

Subsequently, on the day of our official engagement, Khatijah seemed strange. She kept looking at me with the 'not bad' expression, as odd as it was. She had small eyes, and a big straight nose in proportion to her small face. She had natural tanned skin, and thin small lips that always looked locked together, with a tiny mole on it. She rarely smiled to show her teeth. She had some moustache that she never wanted to remove, even after Adam asked her about it. A heart shaped face, easy to remember, because she sometimes liked to sharpen her chin to be pointed out when she's talking, or waiting for a response. The 'not bad' expression was the only look she ever gave me every time it was my turn to talk. It was quite awkward for me, but I kept it cool, especially because Adam couldn't look. He kept his head down most of the time.

It didn't even feel very pleasant, to me. Maybe just on the surface. Adam and I finally had our families meet for the first time on that day, but Khatijah was making Adam not attend the engagement at all. I thought it was possible that Adam would have been trying to feel better from that and it was hard for him to. On that day itself, Khatijah told Adam that he didn't have to be there for the engagement. She wanted him to go to class, of all days that he has been skipping his classes anyway. I was confused about that. I made him go, because my side of the family and I thought it would be odd if they don't even get to know who he is. They never met him before. It was odd that they wanted to have the engagement on a day that Adam would potentially have to be unavailable. They could have postponed it much earlier instead. There was no traditional exchange of gifts during the engagement, either. It was just tea time. This was all from the request of Khatijah, according to real Islam, as she said.

Before I joined them in their discussion, Khatijah was rude to my family about following the 'Sunnah', which is the Prophet's way. She didn't care to hurt their feelings about the marriage traditions they were excited about for me to experience. I knew that there's a way to kindly correct people, especially according to Islam, but she didn't watch her condescending, offensive tone at all. (I learned it the worst throughout the entire marriage, of the horrible tones she liked to use.) Luckily, my family was very patient and kind about it, and they accepted what had happened. After all, they said that if I'm happy, then they're happy. However, since then, it was hard to forget the lasting impression of the so-called 'Sunnah', yet non-diplomatic, ways.

Adam wanted us to be married as soon as possible, so we only had two months of the engagement period. During this period, when we were hanging out at my place, we talked about the headscarf.

He asked me, "Would you ever wear a headscarf?"

I thought about it for a while, imagining myself.

Then I said pensively, "Yeah… I've thought about it… At the end of my journey, I imagine it to be really beautiful… With my lover. Yes, I'd wear a headscarf one day." I nodded.

I went to my mom's that same week and I found some scarves I got as gifts. I met Adam on another day back at mine and I surprised him with one of them on lightly, for fun.

I was laughing, excited that I surprised him.

"I'm just trying it out," I said to him.

He acted pleased at first, but he was mostly indifferent to it the rest of the time we were out. I wasn't all that used to it, but I was excited and having fun with it on. Then when we got back to mine, I removed it.

Adam was sitting on my bed, looking up at me while I was standing. I was facing the mirror that was in front of us. I looked at him. He was so shocked seeing me, like he hadn't seen me in a long time, and he was speechless. He stared at me like he was aroused and emotional at the same time. His breathing was intense. I stared back at him, eyes wide, amused, and smiling. He pulled me closer to him slowly for me to sit with him. He closed his eyes, leaned his head on me, and hugged me for a very long time. It was a very sweet moment.

Suddenly, for the rest of our engagement period, Adam became just the opposite of what happened. He would express his appreciation of me wearing it, a lot more than when I wouldn't. I didn't understand what happened. He would suddenly be emotionless when I would not have it on. I started feeling uneasy, and a little pressured by him. My mood was low. He left for holiday in New Zealand, then came back in the last month of our engagement period.

I continued to see him with it on lightly over my head every time, and he was very happy. He was the happiest then. His face was bright. His attention was fully fixed on me. I still wore it on and off, though, because almost none of my existing clothes at the time were suitable clothing for the Islamic headscarves.

I realized this when I was wearing my tights and he told me to just remove it. I thought it was funny. I felt cool with the headscarf over me, regardless. I felt bold. But I knew I had to build up a new wardrobe if I wanted to keep wearing the scarves. Soon after, I got rid of most of my clothes because they were of no use for me anymore. Most of them stopped sparking joy. I decided to spend a few thousand bucks on some new pieces of more suitable clothing for the scarves. I entered a new world of shopping, one I had never done before. I was looking for 'Muslimah' (meaning, Muslim woman) clothing online. The ones I found were mostly easy slip-ons and long sleeved maxi dresses. They looked classy and stylish. I became excited with the change. I was making big, spiritual change to my life. All the shopping made me feel I was ready.

The wedding was on 23rd March, 2014. It was so simple, to make it as Sunnah as possible. I didn't even have wedding makeup on, as requested by them. No eye-shadow, no eyeliner, no contouring, none of the usual makeup for weddings. All I had on was some light mascara, natural toned powders and some natural toned lip gloss to moisturize my lips. Everything else was so simple, too, but I still loved how it all turned out. It was so beautiful, as arranged by my mom, her family and friends. It was at my late-grandparents' place, and I had my cousin Elsa's stunning wedding dress on and some accessories that she let me borrow, too. I couldn't have arranged it better with all the simplicity, thanks to my mom and family.

After everyone was done eating and taking photos, shortly the wedding was over and everyone left the wedding. We then started taking our wedding photos. Adam was randomly acting impatient about it, without warning, telling me to quickly be done with it. We had literally just started, though. I didn't understand it. But then I faintly remembered seeing Khatijah leave, as I saw others left, too. She was looking down as if upset about something. It seemed as though he was worried about where his mom could be. But Adam was twenty-six years old at the time, and it was his first day as a married man. My first thought was, *'Why is he acting like a child?'*. I was so worried by the thought. He continuously behaved that way throughout the entire photo session. I was deeply offended by it, considering everything that day was professionally arranged and paid for by my mom, but I chose to be patient with him. I sympathized him instead, for being an only child. That's what I thought the problem was.

3

HOME SULK HOME

It was a calm, beautiful day. We were from the wedding, on the way to Khatijah's two-storey terrace house that was our home. It wasn't my first time being at the house. I've been there, before marriage. Adam snuck me in at night sometimes, and I've spent a few days there when Khatijah left for holiday. Adam also invited me to meet Khatijah at the house during a religious class, and I moved in all my things to the house within the last few days before the wedding.

The interior was plain, with uncolored walls displaying beautifully framed Arabic art. The flooring downstairs was of marble texture with Persian rugs. Furniture didn't come as a set, but they were mainly wooden, mostly antique in design. Living room table was of glass top to display some plates with Arabic Art. Cream colored pillows and big polka dotted pillows on the cushioned, wooden sofa bench. Basic bathrooms like they were never remodeled after buying the house. The stairs, and all over upstairs, had the oldest type of wood flooring I had ever seen. They were the size of narrow chocolate bars, in parquet, and they liked to grab onto my feet sometimes and fly off somewhere else when I walk. Connecting the pieces of wood back into the floor easily became a normal thing to do.

There was a glass sliding door covering the entire wall of the living room, facing the humble garden outside. It had bamboo blinds in front of it, on the outside. It was normally rolled up, showing off the garden. It was my favorite part of the house. I would sit there to do work or just appreciate the garden. Most of the time when no one was home. I wanted to take care of the garden sometimes, watering it at least, but Khatijah never liked that.

Adam's bedroom door was covered in heavy duty cellophane tape all around the sides. There were cracks all over, like it could be peeled off easily and things could be stored inside. The whole thing looked like it was just a cream colored wood plank plastered on a wall, with some black boyish stickers all over it. (Later on I added some Barbie stickers.) The entire knob set was weak and looked like it had been broken before. It was always shaky and loose. I just thought it was supposed to be a cool teenage punk room kind of look that he never got around to changing as he got older. He always told me the house was really old, so although I had never seen a door wear out like that, I thought his had worn out.

Adam went upstairs to pack up for our three days, two nights honeymoon my mom got us at the nearest five-star hotel, only ten minutes away from the house. Adam told me we couldn't leave the country because of his mom. It was also rather difficult to persuade him to agree to a honeymoon at all, because according to their views, honeymoons are considered an innovation in Islam. It's not rightly guided, according to them. But I couldn't agree with that. Honeymoons are nice to go for, because it's a relaxing holiday at the beginning of a marriage. My mom also never heard of such a thing.

I stayed downstairs to accompany Khatijah while Adam went up. I was hoping to get to know her more. She sat down on the two-step stairs that divided the living room and the dining area. Without me saying a thing to her, she immediately looked at me in the meanest way, like I just destroyed her life. She held her stare while I was surprised that she did it in the immediate moment Adam left us. It was quite awkward considering how shameless she was about it.

I just continued on smiling at her and talking to her.

She continued staring at me.

"What's that?" I asked, pointing to a box next to her.

She ignored me, still staring at me in the same way, as if wanting me to respond to it.

"Is that an air fryer?" I asked, hoping to create a loving bond with my new mother-in-law.

She turned to look at it, and mumbled, "Yeah." She rolled her eyes to look at her feet, while removing her socks off.

"Do you want me to help you with it?" I asked her, offering to help her set it up.

She ignored me.

I walked closer to her, pointed to the air fryer box, and repeated myself louder, "Do you want me to help you with it?"

I thought she couldn't hear me all of a sudden because of her hearing problems. She was wearing a hearing aid.

She still didn't look at me, but she quietly said while sulking, "Adam will do it."

But we were talking completely fine the whole way home and when Adam was still downstairs. We were happy. I didn't know what I did to deserve that. I chose to be kind and patient about it. I smiled at her, and I went upstairs to get ready for the honeymoon.

The first day of our honeymoon was beautiful. On the second day of our honeymoon, however, right before having late lunch, Khatijah asked Adam to send her to her religious class at her friend's place. There was no planning of it beforehand, no prior notice at all. Adam didn't usually drop her off to her classes, but somehow, according to her, she was finding it difficult to get there as she normally would. She couldn't drive there herself, suddenly. I thought it was odd. But I told him to go and help her, so I would be able to have sushi. I needed to satisfy my cravings at the time, and he hates sushi.

But Adam clearly told me, "I don't wanna go."

I knew he thought it was odd, too. They took about an hour to figure out what to do while on the phone, when we were in front of the hotel. We were at an outside area of a mall, where that was a sushi restaurant. I was too hungry that I eventually excused myself to go in the restaurant on my own and ordered straight away. It would be unfair for me to wait any longer. I was quite annoyed by the disrespect, but I acted indifferent. All I wanted was sushi.

While waiting for my orders, I saw Adam through the glass

window in front of me, still talking to his mom. A few minutes after, he came in the restaurant.

"I don't have to help her anymore," he told me.

Khatijah suddenly changed her mind. It was odd, considering it was our honeymoon and it clearly was nowhere close to an emergency. But we weren't bothered the rest of the time, or at least Adam never bothered to use his phone again. We had a very sweet, relaxing night together as honeymoons should be.

When we got back home the next day, we had to think about the arrangement of our bedroom. It was packed with both our things as we had left it. I knew when I came to bring my things there a few days before, that nothing was prepared like how a newlyweds' bedroom would normally be; beautiful, comfortable, and welcoming. The main furniture were a single bed mattress on the floor, two workout equipment, a study desk, and built-in cupboards on one wall. My things were in separate bags all over the floor.

We wanted to put some of our things in the guest room temporarily to help us get organized, but Khatijah didn't allow any of our things anywhere else in the house. The guest room was a room she never used, but she still got really angry and say we can't use it. But it looked like a store room, anyway. It was filled with dusty, unused things. She didn't even use that room. If we wanted to leave our bags downstairs when we came home, just as she would, she had the same angry reaction and say that it's messy. But the downstairs area tends to be messy with all her things too, just like the guest room, only with no dust.

Adam and I both knew she was being quite odd with the storage space for some reason. My first thought was that my husband was going to feel horrible. It made me feel uneasy. I wanted Adam to feel good and confident about his life regardless of how his mom was, so I continued on treating Khatijah like nothing was wrong with her. I smiled at her every day, and I offered her help every day too, regardless. I tried my best to have a loving bond with her as I had the intention to since pre-marriage. After all, I was prepared to take care of her for the rest of my life.

To make the room more decent and comfortable, we moved the two gym equipment out to the guest room. We were also to go bed shopping soon. We enjoyed sleeping on the single bed together though, for a few nights, until Khatijah made us get the bed. Adam was paying, but she planned to come along with us. It was good news to me that she wanted to spend time with us.

When we got to the shop, bed shopping was quick and easy. I already knew the type of bed frame I wanted, and the type of wood, and color, too. (I took Interior Design when I was in Texas.) After choosing the best I could find, all of a sudden, Khatijah expressed her disappointment.

She sulked, and said, "I would have chosen a lighter color."

It got awkward for a few seconds.

Adam and I knew she had nothing to do with our bed or even our room. She didn't even spend time making the decision with me, but rather just watched me quietly as I discussed with the shop manager. I hoped she wasn't there just to say that. Adam was quiet, he didn't say anything.

I quickly changed the mood and said cheerfully, "Oh really? You like light wood? That's nice too!"

Khatijah's face immediately got serious and looked like she just woke up from a sulking dream. But everything went well and calm right after. We walked around a little bit, and we confirmed our order.

After we got the bed delivered to us eventually, I rearranged the bedroom furniture and I kept my things that had no storage space, to one corner. Then I started serving Adam breakfast in bed. My only concern was that Adam would have something to eat in the morning. It didn't matter how. I was always worried about his health, because men tend to die earlier than women. I lost my father without warning when I was sixteen. He got unwell, but I didn't think he was going to die at all. I wasn't about to lose my husband the same way. I even made Adam promise me that he would stop smoking tobacco. And he did. It was what my mom made my dad promise, too.

Khatijah saw me preparing the breakfasts a few times, but she was silent as she always was with me, even when she was in the kitchen. Then one morning, she decided to talk to me.

"That's a lot," she said, with a certain air of pride for talking to me, while looking at the tray.

"Oh, it's for Adam, too," I said. I was smiling happily, as if there was music playing in my head. I was pleased that she was choosing to be more friendly with me, her daughter-in-law.

She was silent in response, observantly staring at the tray with no expression. I could tell she still wanted to say something, but she didn't. She was distracted in her thoughts. She followed me upstairs as I carried the tray with me. I thought she was going to sit down and watch TV that was just outside our room, as she normally did. But as I opened the door and brought the tray in with me to serve Adam, she followed behind me. He was lying down, just getting up from bed to sit up, as I was serving him.

Before I could turn around to shut the door, I heard Khatijah go, "Whoa!!!"

It shocked us. I turned around quickly. It was quite funny, so I was laughing. It was nice that she wanted to joke and have fun with us. But when I looked at Adam, it was clear he didn't think it was very funny. It seemed like he was just being patient. He looked at her then had his head down calmly. It was funny until she really did, seriously, start to mock him for not getting up to get breakfast himself. She mocked the breakfast in bed, too, as if it was such a big deal, and implied that I was his servant. He didn't respond to her, and she left.

Since then, Adam didn't want breakfast in bed anymore for as long as Khatijah was around. He didn't even feel like getting up for breakfast most of the time. I was offended. I didn't understand why Khatijah couldn't be happy that her son was at least getting some nice breakfast every morning, keeping himself healthy. However, she started inviting him out every other morning since it happened. I was pleased by that. I was invited by Adam sometimes, too, but I didn't go all the time. Regardless, I thought it was great to have a way for them to still spend some time together.

Besides that, Khatijah often asked Adam to do work for her around the house. Which is understandable. He had to do the dishes if there were any left in the sink, and he had to vacuum the entire downstairs every week before the maids would get there. She also needed Adam to do something for her everyday. However, it was so much that Adam was never able to have time to focus on his work or his studies. If I wanted to help her instead, to help lighten Adam's load, she would reject it.

"No, Adam will do it," she would tell me.

I was only able to help Adam when he was there doing the work, such as when he was vacuuming and I would offer to take over. It made me feel horrible that that's all Adam seemed to be doing when he was at home, if he wasn't in the bedroom. I liked that he was helping his mom, but she seemed to be wanting him, and only him, to be exhausted with her demands everyday. Why couldn't I help ease him? Why couldn't he just relax sometimes?

Why?

4

STRIKE ONE

"I'm going for futsal tonight at eight," said Adam, while sitting on his side of the bed with his feet down on the floor. "I haven't gone in a long time. My friends are all disappointed and if I keep ditching then they won't invite me anymore."

Slowly, I asked him, "Oh, are you going alone? 'Cause you didn't invite me."

I was just getting in bed next to him. It was late in the afternoon. I wanted to nap. I didn't actually care if the answer would be a 'Yes' or a 'No'.

"Of course I'm inviting you to go, why would I not want you to?" he answered.

"Aww really…" I said, while giving him a hug. I appreciated that he charmingly took the opportunity to be sweet.

Later on in the evening at 7pm, we were still spending time cuddling. Neither of us were ready to leave. We were both too comfortable. He held me tightly. We weren't moving much, so I figured he was going to end up skipping his futsal again as he has been. I looked at the clock again and it was 7:20pm. If we were really going, I thought, we would have to be out of the house in ten minutes to make it there by 8pm. But Adam was behaving the way he has been with me, so I continued the cuddling too. I didn't want to disturb his rest. I knew from day one that he would get really upset if I wake him up even a minute early.

All of a sudden, ten minutes later, his alarm went off. He turned it off immediately and he got up so fast like he's in the military and started getting ready. He started taking a shower, but he didn't tell me to shower first as I normally would be. I assumed he wanted to take his time anyway. I never thought I could be so wrong. He actually didn't bother at all. Once he was done with his shower, he got ready so quickly that I knew I had no time to catch up. I was being left at home. I didn't care that I had to stay home. I would have gladly anyway. But what got me upset was how he couldn't even tell me that he's sorry for the change of plans. He didn't even bother to say a single thing to me to make me feel better about him having to go without me.

So I acted dumb and I said, "You're waiting for me to get ready, right?"

But all he said was, "I have to go," while rushing around the room looking for things to pack in his sports bag.

I then asked, "Can you wait for me to get ready?"

He repeated himself quickly with, "I have to go, I have no time." He was still rushing around the room looking for things.

It hurt me. I didn't think he would have the nerves to shock me like that. I felt my heart beating faster. I was boiling. I didn't know what I had done to deserve such treatment.

As he walked out the bedroom, I followed him to the stairs and started nagging at him.

"How could you do this? Why couldn't you just tell me?" I asked angrily.

He was ignoring me in every step to the stairs. I grabbed and tugged his bag half way down the stairs to stop him from leaving like a jerk. He resisted. We both fell on our butts immediately. I was on a higher step, and him, lower. Our only connection was his bag that was slightly torn from my pull, and his pull, against the other.

He looked at the tear on his bag and started yelling, "You tore my bag!"

"It's just a bag!" I yelled back in shock.

He repeated in a loud, almost crying whine, "It's torn and you tore it!"

"It's just a bag! I can get you a new one!" I said.

"You tore my bag!" he yelled one last time, as he ran off for his futsal.

I was left on the stairs where I was, shocked and feeling awkward by what just happened. I never knew he could behave that way. I didn't know what his problem was. Why was he so defensive and emotional all the way? What did I do to him? It would've been so simple to just say that he's sorry that the plans have changed. Or at the very least say anything at all, rather than make me feel abandoned and having to question him. It was such an easy problem to manage. I went back in the bedroom.

An hour of silence passed. I thought of all the things I've put up with, all the demands he's had so far. When we would go out together and have normal conversations, especially when it's a debatable topic, he would quickly hush me without me being able to say a single word at all in the entire conversation. At all. It would just be him talking from the beginning to the end. He would point his finger at me like a parent to a toddler, shaking it back and forth towards me, while looking at me with a stern face, warning me not to. The hush, "shh-!" often sounds quick, short and detached, similar to how people would scare off stray cats. The "shh-!" would be quick, but the finger pointing and the stern face would continue for a while longer, both unmoved, watching my moves. If I tried to ignore his hush to just talk anyway, he would continue hushing me every single time in the same way, until he sees that I've gotten tired of it. Then, we would talk about other things as if it never happened. I was never able to say a single word. There was no other way to it. It was almost like a joke, and I would have believed it to be a joke, God knows I wished it was, but it could never be, because I literally was never, ever, ever, able to have a voice in any cases of opposing views. I kept being patient with him and tried to figure out the problem as he was my husband. He was able to get away with saying things like all gays and Hindus should be killed, all the temples filled with idols should be attacked, and other such awful things. I could never have a say at all.

I started messaging him on the phone. Messaging was the only way I was ever able to be heard, unless he would selfishly block me for as long as he wanted to.

I scolded him for whatever it was that happened, saying, "You think it's fine to treat a wife this way? Do you know what a wife means? Maybe you're not meant to be a husband."

I almost concluded that he was stupid. All the ridiculous things he did to me so far would then make sense. And the time he got only one point on an entire major assignment, being two years behind me as well, while I was working on two degrees. I thought he had good excuses for his lack of academic achievement.

I had enough of all that I had to put up with in such a short time in the marriage. I didn't get any response so I waited for his futsal to be over, and I called him. He didn't answer. I called again, and still no answer. He wrote back via a messenger app.

Adam: I just got done.

Me: Maybe we're not meant for each other.

Adam: You're overreacting.

But he disrespected me out of the blue, how could I have overreacted? I didn't respond.

He came home and I was quiet. He sat next to me on the edge of the bed, next to the computer.

"I want to spend a nice time with you," he said to me. "We can have dinner while we watch a movie, and then go out for a ride around the area."

"Why did you do that earlier?" I asked.

"I was late," he answered.

"Why couldn't you just tell me anything at all?" I asked.

"I was late, baby," he answered, looking at me in assurance, staring into my eyes.

I decided to think well of him. I decided that he's too embarrassed to tell me he made a mistake as my man. That he's terribly sorry, and he wouldn't want to hurt me. I accepted it.

Later on by the end of our first month together, Adam's burger stall business was closed for good. He was running a car wash by this time, so his hours were still flexible every day. This time, moreover, to the point of not having any work besides some meetings and just closing up on most days.

Then without any notice at all, he brought home two big sealed bags of white and greyish fungus.

"What is this?" I asked, touching and looking around the bags.

"Don't touch it. Shrooms," he answered. "I made some deals for them."

They were magic mushrooms. A hallucinogenic drug commonly consumed for partying, or for spiritual enlightenment. But they looked gross. I had never seen them before they're juiced. I asked him, "Why do we have these... and why should we sell them?"

He started explaining to me how much we can profit from selling them. But we had no financial problems, I thought.

I was silent and I sighed in return. I asked him for details on how the business would be managed, such as the handling of the drugs, and the dealing. He seemed very happy that I was asking questions. I still wasn't interested. I just wanted to know what my life was going to be like from then on.

I was frowning but I was calm with him. "Why do we have to do this?" I asked.

He was immediately so furious, he snapped and nagged, "How are you going to have food that you like, pay for the car, and go on dates? You think we have enough? You think we can eat good food, and have a nice time anytime you want to?"

It was upsetting to see him use me as the excuse to sell drugs. He was still spending on personal luxury items such as his motorbike, his computer gaming, and his e-cigarette vaping. He never mentioned wanting to have more money for himself. Instead, the horrible economy and all that he has to spend, on me, were to blame. I haven't even once asked him to buy me anything at all, and I've already spent thousands of my own money on clothes, which was supposed to be his support, according to Islam. I rarely asked for expensive food either, most of the time foods like that were on me. I would offer to treat him, so that he would actually want to have them.

"Yes, we do..." I said, slowly.

It was an imaginary problem. I didn't tell him that I saw his bank statement once that he left on his desk, too, so I knew how much he had. And I knew that we were both doing fine. Even though I didn't have income, we were both doing fairly well. I knew he was just impatiently wanting more money. He was willing to blame me, his newly wedded wife, who has been using her own money.

Besides, it's completely normal to not have everything as young newlyweds, and to be paying for a lot of things that it can even seem scary. Especially when we're still students, too. I've heard many newlywed stories with similar beginnings when it comes to money. In the end, the financial problem becomes only a small part of the marriage. So I sincerely wasn't worried.

He responded immediately and louder, "How long do you think it's gonna last? We can barely survive. Times are hard, the economy is getting worse..." his voice was irritatingly loud but I couldn't bother listening much, as he went on and on about the economy.

I felt frustrated with his worries. His instant defensive, bad attitude was too much. I was never much the type to tolerate negativities. I'm quite notorious to tell off and then leave anyone I felt wasn't decent enough for me. I also don't believe in worrying about anything much to the point of stress. I've been very broke, to the point of not having proper meals to eat for days. And I've had a lot of money, too, buying luxury items for friends who never even appreciated them. Both were just fine, in the end. Things turned out well while I was patient. Which was also how I was able to have faith in quitting all my previous jobs, which Adam had requested, even though it was not easy to. Adam and I, in this case, definitely had enough money to at least not be fighting about it.

"Don't worry. Do you want money? How much do you want?" I said, as he listened quietly. I continued, "I can pay for our food, what do you wanna eat?" I needed him to trust that we had no financial problems at all.

"You don't get it. You think it's so easy. Times are hard! People have no jobs! The economy is getting worse! Everyone, even people with money are affected!" his tone was nasty as he went on about it again. He was sitting on the bare wood floor by then, organizing some of his work material.

"But if everyone is affected, then isn't it homogenized?" I asked. "That means there's no difference. No one should be worried at all," I suggested.

There must be some conspiracy involved, if *everyone* was truly affected, right?

He moved his head back with a sigh and said, "You don't get it. Everyone is struggling! People are getting fired!"

I was done rationalizing his weak excuses. I had enough of the discussion and I was so sure I wouldn't accept him dealing drugs. I felt angry with his attitude.

I told him sternly, "I didn't agree to this. You didn't discuss with me first. I don't want 'em in the room, and I don't even want 'em in my sight. I'm not helping you... I never saw this. And I have nothing to do with this." I pointed to a bag of shrooms.

He was offended by my disagreement. "Well it's too late now. There's already a deal," he said, while still organizing his things on the floor, not looking at me.

"What deal? Since when? Why didn't you ask me? Deal with drug dealers but not your wife? You make deals with other people first and then force me to accept them? You do the opposite? I'm forced to accept everything? Now I have a drug dealer husband out of nowhere?" I nagged with questions. It was my first time being able to blurt out so much sense into him.

"Shut up, bitch!" he yelled.

I was never much a fan of cursing, especially when it's at me. How rude of him.

"I'm a bitch...? And I have to shut up...? We're gonna support drugging people...?!" I raised my voice in anger.

He debated against it, telling me how shrooms are good. I didn't mind the debate. I normally would welcome it, except that we were fighting. It's not like he was being nice at all. We went on debating against each other for what seemed like just a single minute, as he moved to the swivel chair in front of the computer. Then he suddenly stopped talking, got up from his seat, and walked to where I was, a meter away from him. He got right in front of me and aggressively pushed me back. I held on to him in defense. He immediately started elbowing me and hitting me repeatedly, hitting my head and body, as I fell down on to the bed.

I felt a blood rush and heat rising up to my face. I sat up and I said with sureness, "I want a divorce."

"No," he said.

I looked at him straight in the eyes and repeated myself sternly, "Divorce me. I want a divorce."

"No," he said.

I ran out of the room looking for Khatijah. It was perfect timing that she just got to the kitchen, too. I saw her walking there as I was going down the stairs.

The moment I got to her, I straight away told her while catching my breath, "Adam hit me so I want a divorce."

She was looking at me, and her face immediately brightened up. It was the first time she was ever happy with me when we were alone together. She pulled herself together quickly, and looked away while she opened the fridge door to search for food.

She nodded while facing the fridge. She squatted down in front of the fridge to continue searching, and said, "Yes, if he hits you, then you should divorce."

Abuse seemed to be so normal for her. She immediately got some fruits from the fridge, served it on a plate, and left me alone in the kitchen. She went upstairs to give the fruits to her son, who she knew just abused me.

I felt uneasy by what she did. While she was preparing the fruits, I thought she would have more to say to help me, but there was nothing. I thought about all the beautiful mothers I looked up to in my entire life. My mom, my aunts, my friends' moms. All their faces flashing in my mind in seconds. I couldn't picture them reacting the same way. I saw them all upset with their sons, making sure they understand not to hurt women. Khatijah was supposed to be one of those moms, too, but she wasn't. It felt even worse that she was my mother-in-law.

I remained calm, and I chose to be patient with her. I was thinking, as I walked out the kitchen to go upstairs, maybe I'm overreacting. Maybe it's normal to fight like this in a marriage. After all, we only had about a month of marriage so far. Maybe things will be better for us. So I gave Khatijah the benefit of the doubt. And I chose to let it go.

I invited Dee, my cousin, over to the house for dinner after that. She was talking about a conflict that happened with a woman who was being difficult at her office. I was trying to find a rational explanation as to why the woman was being that way.

Then referring to me, Dee told Adam, "She always defends bad people."

Adam kept his head down with no response at all to it.

It was quite awkward.

Did Adam know I was hopelessly thinking well of him or his mother?

5

LIMELIGHT JUNKIE

It was a regular day for me when I had to go out to uni. The semester was almost over. Anyhow, all of a sudden, Khatijah started acting like I wasn't supposed to go anywhere. She saw me leave the house many times before, but this time it was different. I was on my way out of the house when she was in the kitchen. She stopped whatever she was doing in the kitchen and she walked fast towards me. She was panicking.

"Where are you going? Where you going?" she asked in a rush, repeatedly, while she hurried over for my answer. She was busy in the kitchen and she was still holding a knife in her hands.

"I'm going out," I said loudly, as she was standing a few meters away from me.

"Where? Where?" she asked persistently.

"To uni," I answered in a similar way, and I smiled at her. I never got a smile back.

"Okay," she nodded slightly and returned to the kitchen.

This exact thing repeated just about every time I wanted to go out. I started giving her the same answers every time, too, just so it would match the routine she was demanding for.

"Where are you going? Where you going?"

"I'm going out."

"Where? Where?"

"To uni."

If I got away with leaving the house without her knowledge, the same thing would still happen. It would be the same, but in a more suspicious manner. She happened to be at home and downstairs when I came back one day. Normally she would be in her room or watching TV upstairs.

Suspiciously, she repeatedly asked me, slowly, "Where were you...? Where were you...?"

"At a meeting," I answered with a smile.

This, too, continued on as a routine every time I came home and she was there to greet me. But she never did any of this to Adam, even if he wouldn't tell her. She would just message or call him later on to ask him. Why did she do this? I have no idea, other than her making my stay there uncomfortable.

If I were to go out with Adam to accompany or support him through his activities, however, such as his futsal or to run errands, she would then focus on bothering Adam, with no care at all that I was there in front of her too.

"Does she have to go too?" she liked to ask him, sarcastically.

Another time, she asked him sarcastically, "She's playing too?"

Adam was dressed appropriately to play futsal, while I was clearly wearing a dress and a headscarf.

"Yes, I'm the striker, you didn't know?" I answered her with a smile.

She couldn't answer me and her face turned serious with a frown. She turned around to leave us as she normally did after her remarks.

It wasn't easy for me to go in and out of the house whenever I wanted to, even if Adam was completely fine with it. I had important things to do, too. It was difficult for me to have freedom and independence, as it would always feel like Khatijah was obsessively stalking me.

Her obsessions didn't stop there.

I just got back home one day. She was sitting in the dining room, sitting in the last chair, facing me. She never sat there before. She usually sat on the first chair, facing the opposite wall that wouldn't have her facing me if I entered. She looked very serious, as if mentally prepared to have a talk with me. I was still in the living room.

"You need to wear an inner hijab," she said to me. An inner hijab is what's normally worn to cover all the hair under the headscarf, to be sure that every strand of hair is hidden.

"Ohhh," I answered her calmly, with my eyebrows raised and nodded. I didn't know why she was acting funny. It just seemed silly to me. She couldn't stop staring at me. That's all she was doing.

Since then, her main (if not the only) topic she talked about was for me to wear an inner hijab. She started talking to me regularly, but criticizing was the only type of talking she had with me when we were alone. It was always about how I was dressed, even when I was in casual wear at home. I wore shorts and tank tops a lot of times, and she told me that they're so sexy, every time, in a condescending, judgmental way. She stared directly at my cleavage to make me feel uncomfortable. She held the stare for a long time, while she was directly in front of me, or just a foot away next to me. There was never a way out of the awkwardness, with the persistence she had about it. She consistently stared into my cleavage in a jealous way, as if inspecting it for further analysis. It didn't matter to her that it was obvious or awkward at all.

I didn't know I had to wear an inner hijab. I thought I had the freedom to dress however I wanted to, following my own spiritual journey, just as I agreed with Adam. I only had the scarves at the time. Some days I wore it on lightly, and some days it would be pinned up neatly, depending on the type of headscarf that I had or what I was wearing. Regardless, out of respect for Adam's wish for me to be covered, I didn't purposely show my hair off anywhere. My hair was casually tied up in a ponytail or in a bun, depending on my mood. Adam never said a thing about me dressing up wrongly. So long as I had a scarf over my head, he was happy about it.

However, Khatijah was persistent in telling me to wear an inner hijab every time she saw me. Even when I was relaxing at home. I noticed her observing me shamelessly with judgmental, critical eyes, whether we were in the house, or out. She stared at my clothes, and she watched my body as I was walking. She wouldn't look at anything else and she was sure to show me. This went on throughout the entire marriage.

One day, I was wearing a light chiffon beige dress that reached my ankles, with a brown belt buckle around my waist. It had some red floral patterns at the top part and on the sleeves. I had a brown hooded scarf on that matched my brown belt. The scarf was in a shape of a hood. It was very easy to wear, as I would put it over my head, then crossed the remaining fabric over my shoulders.

We just got back from having breakfast, on one of the rare days I joined them. I was wearing an inner hijab finally by then, and I hid all my hair in before using the hooded scarf. However, she still wasn't satisfied with it. Adam was waiting in the house, listening, and watching. I was outside the house with Khatijah. She was in front of me by the door. The door was opened and I could see Adam from the corner of my eyes to my right.

"You need to wear a specific type of inner hijab. It should cover the sides of your cheeks, and your chin, too," she said, pointing to the areas on my face. "I'll show you," she said, while looking down. "I have one, I'll give it to you," she added, while organizing some things on the top of the shoe rack. But I rarely ever saw anyone wearing it like that, and I had never seen a single female in her family wearing it like that either.

My eyes widened. I looked at her wondering what she meant. What else about me is she so obsessively unsatisfied about this time?

"What...?" I asked her slowly, confused.

"It's the correct way, you're not allowed to have your face out that much. I have it upstairs, I'll give it to you," she said, while looking at me then looking down quickly, avoiding my eyes. She continued to fix the shoes in front of the door with her feet. Why was my covering not enough? Why was I the only woman that had to have special covering?

"What do you mean...?" I asked, still confused.

She stopped fixing the shoes and immediately acted like I had upset her. She shook her head slightly, frowning.

"Just wear the inner hijab, listen to her," Adam said in annoyance as he showed up at the door. He seemed to have thought I had done something to upset her. Why would I want to do that to my own mother-in-law? I ignored it.

"But why?" I asked to anyone who would answer.

"Just listen to her, wear it," Adam said again, sternly. I couldn't believe he was agreeing so blindly. It turned me off, knowing he was supposed to be the leader of my home, according to Islam, but yet, he was quite empty-headed, I thought.

I never saw Khatijah wear that specific inner hijab they were forcing me to wear, and she wasn't even wearing that type even at that very moment, so I asked her, "Why don't you wear that?"

"I wear a hearing aid, it's uncomfortable… it's not easy," she answered quickly, prepared with her defense, while pointing to her ears.

"Isn't it the new kind? Small, and it sticks to your inner ear lobes?" I asked, remembering her upgrading it. Regardless of the type, though, it just didn't make sense to say that women with hearing aids could wear an inner hijab, but just not that particular one. Either way, the fabric would still have to be touching the ears, wouldn't it?

"It's uncomfortable," she said again, with a desperate, whining expression. I saw her using that expression before, to get Adam to listen to her with no logical explanation. It's sort of like an expression of self-pity. Almost crying-like, as if embarrassed to tell any more than what she's willing to. And she would get away with it. I always knew it was emotional manipulation. I knew what was happening, but I knew a direct confrontation of it would not go well.

"Wear it," Adam said and nodded at me. He ushered me in and guided me to go upstairs with him.

I was then given the specific inner hijab from Khatijah. And I had to buy more of that specific type of inner hijab, too, to be able to wear it regularly. It was supposedly the only right one to wear. I still never bought the weak excuse Khatijah gave.

She continued on being controlling and manipulative about all matters of religion. Or at least, she would claim it to be so. From my appearance, my dressing, to certain prayers and rituals to do, and anything random she would choose to pick on, control, or criticize.

Ironically, one day, when Khatijah stepped out of the car to get some fruits at the shop by the road, she had her headscarf up over her hair, exposing her new, hennaed red hair, that was tied up in a pony tail.

I pointed it out to Adam, "Hey, mummy's headscarf."

He said, "Oh, okay." He acted indifferent, as if it was something normal for her to do.

I didn't understand that, so I said, "I think she would appreciate it if we told her."

"Okay," Adam said. He got out of the car and told her.

Soon after, Khatijah came in the car before Adam and said, "Thank you for that." I sensed aggressive energy from it, but I didn't think anything of it.

"No problem!" I answered back with a smile. She got herself comfortable in the car and I asked her, "By the way, is it okay to wear it high and thick like that?" I asked Khatijah about her high ponytail that was wrapped with a thick, fabric covered elastic hair tie. She once told me that I couldn't tie my hair up high, or make it appear thick under the headscarf.

"Yeah, what's wrong with that? It's better than not wearing socks," she told me.

I never got to the extent of wearing socks everywhere like she was, so she was clearly intending to compare with me.

Adam got in the car and buckled up.

"I thought we weren't supposed to have our hair up like a camel. So maybe that's worse," I told her. The 'camel' head under the headscarf was a sign of arrogance. She even specifically sent me the information in a photo before. I immediately went through my phone to look for what she sent to me.

"Not wearing socks is worse," she said.

"Why? I think the hair thing is worse," I said. Because no one has ever sent me anything about socks.

"To each his own," Khatijah said. "To each his own," she repeated herself.

"Yeah, okay," I agreed, even though I didn't understand how it got to that. I just wanted us to discuss peacefully. She didn't like that it was so easy for me to be at peace with what just happened, though.

"Anyway, how do you know the camel is worse than no socks?" she asked defensively all of a sudden.

"Yeah, how do you know?" Adam joined in aggressively.

"I don't... that's why I'm discussing..." I said to them slowly, confused. I couldn't believe how aggressive they were in such a simple conversation.

"Well, I guess I won't see you in heaven then," Khatijah said to me, seriously, while looking at me.

I immediately got so appalled by her attitude that I couldn't even bother to respond anymore. I just chose to be patient and I sat back.

"Adam, let me drive," she said to Adam, with a serious and arrogant expression.

They both got out of the car to switch seats and Khatijah started driving aggressively. Adam went to sleep straight away. I cried at the back silently, frustrated by how I ended up with such unsophisticated people. I met Adam at a private university, so I thought that at the very least he would have come from a well-educated family.

Khatijah also made it clear a few times that she believed Muslim women are only women who wear headscarves. Women who don't were only considered ignorant or non-Muslim, to her. She made Adam believe it, too.

"If you know Islam, then where's your headscarf?" she once asked the maid next door, Kak Wati.

I was shocked to hear that. I felt bad for the maid. It was very insulting, considering my own mother was amongst the many Muslim women I knew who chose not to wear it. How one dresses should be a personal choice rather than something to be imposed on or discriminated for. A Muslim woman named Fatima al-Kubra, a great descendant of the Prophet, also chose not to wear the headscarf in her daily life. Many other Muslim women followed her the same, too. She was never condemned for it. She was still known as a Muslim. She had human rights and she was always accepted. She was still treated fairly, and still an equal to others.

Besides, the issue of hijab isn't just for women, but for men, as well. I see gender discrimination when I keep hearing both men and women the same, looking down on Muslim women who aren't covered up. They do so to the point of accusing uncovered Muslim women of not understanding Islam, and worse, not being true Muslims. I see more pain in uncovered Muslim women, living amongst such people. It's a terrible mental disease.

Today, Muslim men wear regular clothes on one day, wearing shorts or tight tops, showing off the shape of their bodies, and just about never lowering their gaze around women. They could even have photos of naked women who are strangers, saved in their phones. I see them lifting their shirts, rubbing their hairy bellies held by their exposed groins. Then on another day, they wear a jubah to go to the mosque. No one says anything about that, do they? But some Muslim women, specifically the covered ones, are only allowed to wear what they would if they were to go to the mosque. Wherever they go, they are only able to dress up like they are ready to pray. If she even so much wears her headscarf over her head lightly, she is immediately susceptible to harsh judgments and criticisms. Such as what I had experienced from Khatijah.

She continued to freak out every time I stepped out of the house quickly for anything without a headscarf on. It was a bright, sunny day, with mine and Adam's laundry drying outside. She happened to be downstairs with me too, when I wanted to bring them in. They were just right in front of the door. I was wearing a short sleeved t-shirt. White, with some yellow at the top, adding to the bright day I was having. It wasn't loose, but it wasn't too tight, either. I had a white maxi skirt on with it down to my ankles. My hair was tied up in a low, messy ponytail.

As I was opening the door, I heard Khatijah squeal from the dining area. I stopped where I was. I held the door slightly opened with my left hand and I looked at her to my right.

"Where are you going?" she quickly asked.

"I'm pulling the laundry in," I said, opening the door wider and pointing to the laundry in front of me. It was a single metal bar with wheels.

"Where's your scarf?" she asked, while walking towards me.

"I'm just bringing them in from here," I answered. I was quite surprised. She was acting as if she never did this. In fact, she did it every day. She would go around the outside of her house without a headscarf on at any time throughout the day, even further away than what I was about to do. I backed away from the door as she was heading outside at the same time.

"I'll do it," she said. She was wearing a short sleeve, long nightgown. It was very light and thin in material, sticking to her braless chest. She normally wore the same thing every day at home, but in different printed design. She had no headscarf on. As she walked outside, the sunlight shined through her nightgown, revealing the silhouette of her naked body.

She dressed this way every single day. The front door neighbor had bare windows facing us. Other neighbors were busy with daily activities in and out of the house, too. She didn't mind any of this. It was allowed for her, as ironic as it was. It would be ridiculous to say she just didn't realize how she looked like, considering that exact type of nightgown seemed to be her favorite thing to wear. Her bedroom had half of the blinds opened at the top, all day and night.

Her room was always just as bright in the day because of it. The cupboard doors covering one wall of her room were layered with mirrors over them.

I knew she was oppressing me from daily activities at home, just as she was with everything else. But I chose to be patient with her. It wasn't enough for her though. Soon after, she was unsatisfied with me walking around the house because of the bare sliding doors, too.

She controlled the bamboo blinds outside. If she was expecting anyone, she would roll down the blinds first, as if the house was always like that. They were usually only her friends and family. She did this even if they wouldn't come in the house, or if they just wanted to pass something to her quickly.

"Don't walk around here," she said to me, randomly. She got up from her seat to stand in front of me in the dining room. I was about to go upstairs.

"Don't walk where?" I asked, while looking around us.

"All around here," she said, looking around and moving her arms to show me the entire downstairs. "The dining room, the living room…" she continued, like she was reading a list in her mind. "You can't walk around here. Don't be here."

"What? Why?" I asked. I was calm, waiting for her explanation.

"People can see you," she said, with eyebrows raised, and pointing in the direction of the sliding door.

We were still standing in front of each other. I looked outside from where I was, wondering what the difference was. I was already living there for a while, walking around the house the same way.

"What about you?" I asked.

"It's okay for me, I'm old," she said.

"Then why do you have to wear a headscarf at all in public?" I quickly asked, not getting her logic.

"It's okay, I'm old," she said. She immediately walked away fast to leave me there, as if she was occupied with something else. She went upstairs to her room.

I knew I was being lied to. I had never heard of such a thing. She was a middle aged woman who was still healthy, still active, still traveling, still not requiring anyone to feed her, or walk her to her car for her to drive wherever she wanted to, or get her adult diapers if she needed any. I highly doubt older women wearing headscarves were able to expose themselves whenever they wanted to. Telling me that I can't do something that an older woman can, is age discrimination, too, which is against Islam.

Regardless, to avoid any more negativities, and to have some peace, I started to dim the lights at night so that I could at least eat properly in the dining room. The light was dark yellow, as light as a weak table lamp. It felt horrible to have to do that, but I felt quite relaxed in the dim light. I felt cozy, finally able to use the area again. Adam was out having a meeting and wasn't going to be home till later.

Khatijah went downstairs when I just finished my dinner. I was relaxing at the dining table, browsing through my phone. I had my legs up and crossed on one chair. She didn't turn on the lights. She came to me straight away, then leaned in towards me closely to my face.

"Why are you in the dark?" she asked me, with a laugh held back through her voice.

"People can see me here, right?" I asked her, observantly watching her expressions, waiting for her answer.

Her face got serious. She straightened her back to stand up straight, then she leaned her head and neck back to watch me from a normal distance. As creepy as it was, she didn't respond at all. And then she just walked away as if the conversation never happened. It bothered me how she was consistently unhappy to see me positive, and able to cope through her irrationalities. This wasn't consistent, however, as she would always allow it if we were having meals together with Adam. It appears as though she wanted to control when I could or could not use certain areas in the house.

The following week, she started telling me to hide, without prior notice. I was in the kitchen, making dinner for Adam and myself. (I usually offered her too, but she's picky with her diet. She would say 'No' almost all the time.) I had the ingredients prepared out for fried rice and I was preparing some salad.

"Go upstairs, Zahir's here," she said in a rush, as she walked in the kitchen.

"What?!" I asked, surprised. "Why?" I looked at her not believing what she was saying. Adam's cousin was there, and I had to leave my cooking because of that.

"He's getting the banquet tables. Go," she said, still in a rush. The banquet tables were in the laundry room. That's not the kitchen.

"I'll just stay in here," I said. I was too busy. I closed the kitchen door that was glass with mullions. I wasn't standing in the door's view. It was all fine.

She knew that I always liked to use the kitchen. I used it a lot. It should have been expected for me to be preparing meals for dinner, or at the very least it should have been kept in mind. But she didn't bother telling me beforehand at all. It was odd, considering she was a planner. She was clearly the type of person who would spend a lot of time planning. Just as she planned and organized her religious classes and other such events with her family and friends.

It happened again a few times after, when I wasn't busy in the kitchen. She made me hide upstairs repeatedly. It felt so rude. I could have at the very least dressed differently for Adam's cousins instead of having to hide. I was used to living with housemates from many different countries, from my experience of moving around to different residences over the years. None have I ever experienced rudeness such as this. Even more so, she was my mother-in-law. It was even more inconsiderate, to not inform me, especially when something was expected of me every time. I knew she would be persistent in acting dumb, just as everything else so far, so I kept it to myself. I chose to be patient.

Then, one day, something even more unusual started happening. I didn't get ready in my casual wear as I normally would, before going downstairs. I was always uncomfortable to dress up comfortably around Khatijah, because of her persistent staring and remarks, but I just didn't bother at the time. I went braless in my black, short sleeved, Victoria's Secret short nightgown that I got as a gift from my mom.

Khatijah looked at me from the dining table as I walked down the stairs into the living room. I greeted her as I normally would, but she didn't interact with me at all after that. She kept her head down. No looks, no talking. No criticizing. I quickly grabbed some food and went upstairs.

A few days later, Adam took me out for dinner. We were ready to relax for the rest of the night when we came back home. Before we both got to sit down in the bedroom, I got so shocked by what I found.

There were two holes on each sleeves of that very same nightgown I wore comfortably, downstairs, to grab breakfast.

I had chills up my neck. I was speechless.

I held the nightgown in my hands with my eyes wide and my jaws dropped for a long time.

"Uh… What… is this…" I asked Adam slowly, with the same expression. I showed him the two holes.

He looked at them and scratched his head quickly. Then he looked at me. His face was serious and calm, taking note of my reaction.

He sighed.

"Must be Jinan," he said.

Jinan was his cat of six years (at the time) who had problems with eating clothes sometimes. The only problem with that theory, however, is that I had the nightgown hung up high where Jinan couldn't have possibly reached. Unless of course, Jinan was secretly a spider cat that could morph through the cracks of the door, too. But let's be real here.

"How can Jinan reach this…" I asked, still feeling the same.

He shrugged. "Must be from another day," he said.

"No… it was always hung up there…" I said, still so much in shock, pointing to the high hooks on the wall.

He listened and we looked at each other. He was thinking with me. Then he shrugged. He raised his left hand slightly while having a seat in front of the computer, to say, "I don't know."

We couldn't conclude anything about it. Since that happened, I still started finding more and more tears on my clothes. They were mostly the nicer clothes I had. There was a white inner top that I got and it was new, I only wore it once. A brand new Christian Dior satin lingerie robe that was folded in my wardrobe, and some high end casual wears from Gucci and Prada, also were folded in my wardrobe, and some dresses, and such. It was very creepy.

It was always easy for me to be detached with material things, though. I lost my handbag once, with thousands of Singaporean dollars in it, my bank cards, identity card, a camera, and a phone. I didn't shed a single tear. I was a total nun.

However, just because material things can mean nothing to me, doesn't mean that I would tolerate injustice when it comes to it. I completely couldn't find my rugs that had dogs on them anymore. Adam denied anything about that, but of course there was one other person living with us. The damaged and lost things were some of my favorite. It hurt knowing that they all happened in my own home, but I just kept choosing to be patient.

6

MOTHERPULATOR

It was early in the afternoon. I heard Adam come home from work but he didn't come to the bedroom straight away. I could hear him greeting his mom downstairs. After a while, he came in the bedroom acting bothered about something.

I asked, "What's wrong, baby? Is everything okay?" I set aside my laptop to comfort him.

He didn't want to tell me anything, but he still seemed distraught.

I decided to continue on talking to him as if everything was really fine, in the hopes that he would be cheered up.

But it turns out that he was angry. He needed to let out his frustrations on me.

"Why don't you spend some time downstairs?" he asked.

"I don't mind… but I've been doing my work in the room 'cause I've just been comfortable doing it here," I said in all honesty. And I asked, "Why?"

"You should see your mother-in-law sometimes," he said.

"I do, you know, I see her," I answered. Not understanding why he's saying that.

"When?"

"Random times every day. But you're not always here to see when I see her."

He paused to think, as if he expected a different answer. He said sternly, "See her more, she's your mother."

"I know. I see her every day and I talk to her. But she never talks like how normal conversations would be when we're alone," I tried explaining to him without telling him how two-faced his mom really was with her attitude. "And how am I supposed to wait for her to be out of her room or not at her religious classes every time? You want me to camp for the right time..? I have a lot of work to do..."

Again, my answer was not what he wanted to hear and he was annoyed. "She's old, she has no company. She can fall down the stairs," he sounded like he was brainwashed, actually.

It was scary. I've heard him say this a few times before. But I know so many old women who are living their lives like never before. Dancing, traveling, being independent on their own, and more. Hillary Clinton and Martha Stewart, elderly women empowered in their seventies, for goodness sake. My strong paternal grandmother, too, way retired in her eighties. She has all kinds of physical disabilities, yet she embraces and chooses to live alone despite having many options to be dependent. And she can't even drive. Khatijah on the other hand, only sixty-two, was still driving her car, still ran around the house all the time, still had friends at her religious classes, and still goes out to exercise with her family, too! Where was the common sense?

"Then I would run to help her as I *always* do when she makes a loud noise...?" I said, pausing to see if he understood it enough. "I have thesis. Do you know how much work that is? Do you understand what thesis is?" I asked slowly. I was so annoyed with the imaginary problem. It wasn't going anywhere. To top it off, what ever happened to their religiosity? After all the religious classes, where was their trust in God? I was stressed. I grabbed a cardigan over my night slip, and headed for the door in annoyance to go downstairs. "I'm leaving," I said.

He went after me. He pulled me by the hair down to the floor, twisted me around spinning on my butt as I landed sideways. My hands were covering my head, protecting myself in a fetal position. He immediately started beating me while screaming, "You slut!!! You whore! Cover up, you whore!!!" I almost thought he had a sadomasochistic fetish for women in headscarves. He wanted me to be in pain while he insulted his way to dominating me and to cover up. Why did he even think I was being a whore for wanting to leave the room the way I was dressed? What made him think like that?

He continued beating me with, "You don't even know how to speak Malay!!!"

Actually, I do know, but I don't know why he kept treating me like I don't. He's the one that would keep telling people I don't, as well. Just because English is my native language, and I have the tendency to sound a little awkward when I form the Malay grammar or some big words in my mind sometimes, doesn't mean that I should be treated like I'm ignorant with the Malay language, which I do understand and can speak. He knew this, years before we got married. He even knew that I was attending some Malay language classes, both in and out of uni. Private, and local. I even had conversations with him in Malay. What made him say these things to me?

I managed to get myself up when he paused. But he slammed me against the door. He slammed me repeatedly. My head and my back were getting the most of its impact while I blocked my face. It was too crazy, I thought he would stop soon. He grabbed me and pushed me to the floor. I blocked myself in a fetal position as he continued beating me again, screaming, "You hate my mom!!!"

That's when it occurred to me. This had nothing to do with our conversation. This had nothing to do with what I did wrong. I didn't do anything. I didn't insult him, and I didn't ask for a fight at all. In fact, I was running away from the negativities to begin with. I didn't even talk to him for long. Why would he say that I hate his mom? I had done nothing but love her, smile at her every day even with her grumpy face and eye rolling responses back at me. I persevered in honoring her and serving her. I had always only loved her.

I understand that I possibly have an unusual view of love and of family. I loved them unconditionally even when they're not blood related to me, because I've been strongly influenced by my mother's side of the family. My mom's family have adopted siblings. I know how much I loved Adam's mom immediately after she became my mother-in-law, perhaps more than people without such experience of love, or the capabilities of love, could ever understand.

There must be something that Khatijah said to him, I thought. There would be no other possible factors, but that. It would make sense and it would match with her attitude all this while. I was in shock with the awareness. I was so deep in thoughts. I almost didn't feel his beatings over me.

I slowly got myself up again and he immediately pushed me all the way to the nearest wall, in between the bedside table and the cupboard. I was stuck there, unable to move anywhere but forward, where he was. I continued blocking myself, trying to push him back away from me. He was too heavy. He slammed me repeatedly every time my back wasn't touching the wall. He was going fast. I imagined him with a strait-jacket on, and I was the padded cell for him to repeatedly bounce himself against. It was pretty much like that. He was nuts.

There was no way for me to push him back. He was at least twice the size of me. All I could do was block as much as I could, and tell him to stop when I was able to catch my breath. I couldn't take it anymore. I thought I was going to die like that. My back was in so much pain. My vision was shaky and blurry. I couldn't see anything properly as it was happening so fast. I closed my eyes while blocking myself.

I told him to stop but he wouldn't. As I repeatedly told him to stop, he seemed to enjoy it more. He stepped back and I thought it was finally over. I thought I was able to step forward to relax, but no. He grabbed me quickly and pushed me to the cupboards this time. He did the same thing to me there as he did to me on the door, and against the wall. I knew my head and my back were most at risk, so I used all the strength I had left of me to tighten all the muscles I had left in my body. I was in the hopes that I would still be alive and not be physically disabled, either. He slammed me against the cupboard door repeatedly.

Finally, the wooden cupboard door, about eight feet tall, completely broke and was falling on us. He stopped. I was relieved.

Adam immediately lied down in bed and closed his eyes, as if nothing happened. He was in total peace. He was calm, his face was calm, and his breathing was calm. It was as if he was relaxing on a holiday, listening to the sounds of the beach within a second. It felt so creepy as I watched him, wondering if he's spiritually possessed. I had chills up my neck every time I looked at him. Even when I only looked at his legs.

I went to the other side of the bed, crying to myself. My entire body was sore. I was covered in red and purple bruises all over me, and my bones felt as broken as the cupboard door, but I was still alive. I was grateful. I was exhausted.

I gained three things from the attack: betrayal of trust, physical pain, and the awareness of his mom's possible manipulation against me. Adam and I were both quiet for a long time. After a while, I kindly asked him for a divorce.

"I want a divorce," I said.

He was silent.

"I want a divorce," I said again. I repeated myself twice, calmly.

He finally woke up from his dreamland.

"Okay. I divorce you," he said, as he sat up to look at me and left the room in a second.

I was relieved. I immediately grabbed a bag to pack my clothes in. I knew I would have to make many rounds for all my things. It wasn't going to be easy, to trust having my things there without me.

He came back in the room two minutes later and gave a sudden dramatic, horrified expression, watching me so sure to leave him. I didn't bother with him. I continued to focus on my packing calmly as he was staring at me that way. He came over to me, and held my hands gently as I was holding some clothes. I felt disgusted. I pulled my hands away. He was persistent in holding my hands. He tried to stop me from packing, taking over the stuff off my hands.

"Stop, stop," he said. His eyes were focused on me. He gently ushered me to sit down. I looked back at him, puzzled. I felt uncomfortable just looking at him.

"I want you back," he said.

"No," I answered.

"Please!!!" he shouted. He immediately started crying hysterically, tears flowing out like a water fountain that was suddenly turned on.

I couldn't even believe what I was seeing. How could he cry so much about me leaving? He loves me? No one would cry like this for me if they didn't love me, right? It didn't make sense.

"Why are you crying," I asked in a monotone way, not sure if I really cared. I had no feelings for him at all. Nothing. I went through enough to feel anything for him.

He continued crying and asked me kindly, "I want you back, please..."

He stared at me with his eyes flooded in tears, flowing like gentle river. I felt tears slowly filling up my eyes, too. I felt sympathy for his emotional instability. I didn't understand. By then I knew he had deep psychological issues. But I didn't quite know what all the problem was yet. My only clue so far was his mother.

"Please," he cried again, sobbing, "I want you back..."

"No," I repeated myself.

"Why!!!" he cried and stomped his feet, running out of the room. The crying was as if our relationship had been amazing and he wasn't allowed to marry me or something. Him as a three-year-old toddler, though. He ran back in again and quickly kneeled down in front of me in a rush. While catching his breath, he said, "I don't want a divorce. Please, I want you back. I love you. I love you!!!" He cried and yelled with so much passion. He held onto my arms. He lightly yet stiffly, shook me in frustration.

"Then why do you abuse me?" I asked. He started sobbing and choking on his pool of tears that covered his face. He looked down, sobbing, and back at me. "Do you think it's fine to abuse me? Your wife? Are you going to do it again?"

"No," he begged, shaking his head. He looked at me with his face entirely wet with tears and his snot. His lips were shut together, slightly pouting, shaking, spitting overflowed tears and saliva. It was quite gross. I wondered why he tends to do that when he would cry for me to comfort him. He would let his saliva and snot run out like melted string cheese, as if there's a power button for it somewhere. It always bothered me, but he wouldn't care at all, regardless of where all the snot and spit would land. Like a toddler. "I won't," he cried and begged, and moved in closer to me.

I knew he was emotional. But I had no idea the randomness of his emotions went to this extent, to the extent of harming me. He had other excuses for his emotional instabilities before. But he would most definitely always cry to get me back.

I fell for it. I believed him. I felt sympathy.

"Stop crying," I said, while I quickly got a pack of tissues to wipe his face and clean his snot. I always had to clear his nose. I gave him a hug and I rubbed his back to comfort him. He held onto me gently and went in bed with me, as I pet his head and comfort him for the rest of the day.

After that, I stayed at home for a while, healing from all the pain I had. I didn't go anywhere at all, not even to any of our family events, for a while. I didn't care to walk around the house with my dark purple bruises for Khatijah to see, too, but every time I exposed the bruises in front of her, she would ignore me in her view. I had them all over me for more than two months.

I was glad Adam said all that he did when he beat me. It felt like he needed my help, but he just didn't know how to tell me. Obviously it was a very deep problem, as much as he had expressed. I would never forget that.

After that happened, I noticed Khatijah started the tendency to randomly bite her lips in anger, when she saw me in the house. She was also banging on the door every single morning at dawn for us to wake up. Not knocking, but *banging*. Even when we're already awake anyway, with lights on that she should have been able to see around the door. Which was pretty much every morning. It was always dark outside the room in the hall, and I even checked how bright the lights were, shining through the sides. It didn't matter to her though. She would always still be banging on the door like an angry person. It would never even gradually go from knocking to banging. It would just be aggressive banging immediately.

I could tell Adam was very annoyed with her, because he wouldn't continue to be awake. He would instead quickly answer just for the sake of keeping her calm in the morning, then a lot of times he would go back to sleep. She would not stop until the door was opened. If we didn't answer her, she would continuously call Adam's phone, or the home phone that was right next to the door.

She banged on the door, every single morning. Throughout the day, too, she continued to bang on the door every single time we got quiet in the room. Every single time, as odd as it was. If Khatijah was home, and Adam and I were quiet in the room, the door banging was sure to come. I eventually figured that the broken, taped up door was because of her all along. I never before imagined there could be a crazy reason behind it.

7

THE ROOT OF ALL EVIL

Adam wouldn't allow me to do any of the jobs I had before marriage, as they focused on my physical appearance. This also meant that I wasn't allowed to be active on social media anymore, and I wasn't allowed to take photos at all, either. The only photos I was ever allowed to take of myself were ones of him in them, too, or with family.

I continued getting modeling offers, but I wasn't able to accept them. Of course, with a headscarf on, I was unable to anyway. He didn't want me working nine-to-five to be a corporate slave, either, as he liked to say. He told me to use my savings first for a while. Because of the change in my work life, and I was never used to not working, I chose to run a waffle catering.

Adam surprised me with a commercial waffle maker that he found online, at first. It was used, but it made me feel so touched and surprised that he was really helping me with work. I thought it was very thoughtful of him. It showed his sincerity in helping me, I thought. Then, he exchanged it with a new one, because he realized it was too hard for the used one to be cleaned.

I made the waffle batter when only Adam was home. I was sure to have the kitchen spotless immediately after, as I normally did after cooking. Khatijah came home from a religious class and saw the prepared batter on the dining table. She scanned around, searching for more things. She was walking from the kitchen to the dining room repeatedly, making it obvious that she was doing so.

Then she said in a low voice like something terrible just happened, "Ohh… you need to get your own kitchen."

"Why?" I asked, standing next to her, surprised. We were by the kitchen door.

"You need to get your own kitchen," she repeated herself, without looking at me.

"Why?" I asked, louder, thinking she had problems with her hearing aid.

"Adam, don't forget this weekend," she ignored me.

Adam had a pause to his reaction at first, then said, "Okay." He was standing in front of her, then he nodded, while awkward with the situation. I was right next to them.

"Why do I need another kitchen?" I asked again, loudly. I was directly right next to her.

"I've already answered them so don't forget," she ignored me again and continued talking to Adam. Then she walked away to go upstairs.

This happened repeatedly, every time she saw some prepared waffle batters on the dining table. This was what she did every time I needed an answer. It was just as routine as everything else she was oppressing me from. It ended up being too annoying to deal with to the point of Adam encouraging me not to continue with a big private event I was invited to for the catering. I was the only new business amongst known companies involved. I continued getting more private inquiries, too, but I had to tell everyone that it's been put on hold, to the point of stopping my business operations entirely.

Meanwhile, Khatijah continued to randomly tell me to do charity work with my waffle catering instead, alongside the routine of asking me disdainfully, "No work?", "You don't have a job?", "You're still not working?", and along those lines, throughout the entire marriage. Her jealousy for the success of my business was just about transparent to me, considering she was trying to do well with her sisters in selling pasta from home.

Not long after, Adam sulked about it like it was a burden he ever bought the waffle maker for me, reminding me that he has spent on me. I thought of offering him back all that he had spent for both of the waffle makers, but the waffle maker was supposed to be a gift, like he said, so I thought it would be awkward.

Instead, I promised him, "If I ever make some profit with the waffle maker, there will be no end to thanking you. Even if I expand my business using that profit, I'll still always be thanking you. I promise to God, you *will* get more than what you have ever given me, if I do well with this waffle maker."

I would have gladly given him free money as if he was a silent partner, if I ever did do well. It was in my plans, anyway. It was one of the things I wanted to surprise him with, along the way in the marriage.

I used to read a lot of inspirational stories as a child, of those who once had nothing, and one day became rich, then showing gratitude to someone who once gave them a glass of water when they were thirsty. A doctor sending the patient a receipt, saying, "Paid with a glass of milk", and such dramatic stories. I've always wanted to do that to someone. I thought Adam was going to be this "Thank you for the waffle maker" guy, for me. It sounds silly now, especially since I never even asked him to buy the waffle maker for me. He chose to surprise me with it. But it could have still been possible, right?

The first time ever in the history of my relationship with Adam that I had asked him to buy me something, was when I had to buy some new headscarves. I only had about ten, and of the ten, there were only about five pieces for casual wear to mix and match with whatever dresses that I had bought before marriage. That was all I had at the time, so I clearly still didn't have much to wear. Anyone that saw me every day could easily tell my wardrobe was limited. Although, I was so busy with research for my Honors thesis and my waffle catering operations I was running, that I didn't feel like going out unless I had to.

I still wasn't used to the 'Muslimah' shopping. It was a different world of shopping to me. I quickly stopped by a small hijab shop in the parking lot where Adam, Khatijah, and I, ran some errands and had lunch together. I found two basic colored scarves that could be used for many occasions. One was cream colored, and the other one, navy blue. Both had simple, feminine floral lining on one side. Adam agreed from outside the shop and gave me money for it. After paying, I left the shop, walking with Adam over to Khatijah, who was facing me. I was so happy, I held a broad smile at her.

I showed her what's inside the bag and I said, "I just got some scarves!"

She looked at the bag quickly, then looked at me and said, "You have money, right?" and quickly walked away.

I was shocked she said that, considering in Islam, it should be the husband's responsibility to provide clothes for his wife. I thought she was religious.

For the rest of the marriage, I had to continue on shopping for clothes using my own money, because Adam couldn't afford to. I was given allowance once in awhile, but only after I would get abused, and only if I asked for it, which ended up being no more than a hundred ringgit per month of allowance throughout the entire marriage. One hundred Malaysian Ringgit per month for everything I needed to get, throughout the entire three years. This included all my clothes, my food and drinks when I had things to do outside the house, any fees, medications, supplements, and any kind of doctor visits, *unless* I told him it's for a pregnancy check-up (only later on at the end of our marriage). I had no income, and I was living on my savings.

When my mom wanted to be sure that Adam was stable enough to be my husband, she made it clear that she also wouldn't be paying for my remaining college fees anymore. She asked Adam if he really can be responsible for me.

It was night time. We were at my mom's, in front of her pantry. My mom was standing at the pantry door, keeping away some things. Adam and I were in front of her, facing the pantry.

"Are you sure you can pay for the remaining college fees?" my mom asked him.

"Yes," Adam said and nodded.

"Are you sure? You can be responsible for her and even pay for her remaining college fees?" she asked, while looking at Adam observantly, and her hand moving slowly to reach the door behind her without looking at it.

"Yes, I'm sure," Adam said, and nodded his head in assurance.

That's when my mom was finally more comfortable about me marrying him. She was sure he was an independent, grown man. He was able to afford being responsible for me, so it made her feel safer to agree.

I thought there were only two subjects left, at first. By the time I was done with my thesis, I was informed by the uni department that I still had three more subjects to complete. Adam was sulking about the three additional subjects so much that I offered to pay for everything back entirely. That was a total of five subjects for 7000 ringgits. He shook his head to tell me 'No'.

However, he wouldn't pay for any extra fees at all. I still had to pay for them myself. He wouldn't even pay the late penalty fees he made me end up paying, after abusing me, and convincing me that it would be fine to pay late. I was patient about it, but I thought he might as well have told my mom that, "Yes, I can pay for the rest of her college fees, but only if there are only two subjects, and only if I don't pay for all the extra fees she has to pay, and all the penalty fees from me abusing her and holding her back from submitting her assignments, too. Also, only if I don't really treat her well with my responsibilities. And she can't work at all, by the way, she will always have to depend on me, even if I won't actually be sincere about supporting her. And I will sulk about everything, regardless."

On the other hand, while saying he didn't have enough money for me, Adam was not only spending on luxury items for himself, but he was hanging out at coffee shops in the area every day, buying coffee and bottles of water throughout the day from the convenience store just next door, and bringing them home. He could have had water from the water dispenser at home, or I could have made him a cup of coffee myself. He knew it, because I would tell him, but he just couldn't stop the habit, prioritizing personal luxury and convenience over his responsibility.

Also, as if it wasn't enough for Khatijah to hate the fact that her son had a wife to spend on, she was literally demanding to go through my things without my permission. The first time she did it was when I came home with Adam one day after shopping, using my own savings.

We were walking past the gate, on the driveway. She came out of the house immediately out of nowhere, as if she had been waiting by the front door. She ran towards me with a forced smile, excited like there was a silent laugh at the same time.

It went so fast and I was so shocked I couldn't even scream if I wanted to. She went straight for my shopping bags, trying to grab them, trying to get a peek, and said, "What did you get? What did you get?"

It was rude to me. I had the immediate reaction to pull the bags away from her like they were my dogs about to bite her, and said, "No!"

How could she habitually express her hate of me shopping, and her hate of her son fulfilling his responsibilities of supporting me, and then all of a sudden think a few seconds of faking a smile, running towards me in desperation is supposed to make me show what I just bought? How egocentric was that?

She continued trying to, and I still kept the bags away from her. She was chasing me around quickly on the driveway in a circle. I never would've thought it would come to that. I've never done that in regard to my shopping before. Or anything at all, for that matter. I was always open to sharing with others.

Adam was quiet, watching. Not really knowing what was happening to his mom, probably. He continued walking calmly as I followed him into the house. Khatijah followed behind me, somewhat laughing to herself while catching her breath, acting like what happened was normal.

As with everything else, that wasn't enough for her. She continued asking me about every shopping I did, which was at least once a month. I remained patient with her, as she continuously mocked me and every purchase I made.

8

KITCHEN GUARD DOG

I started cooking when I was seven years old. My mom had just given birth to my younger brother. Her helper wasn't around at the time, and we were home alone. It seemed like my mom had so much going on with her. I didn't understand it, but I knew she couldn't get out of bed. I was rarely around her during that time. I was always uncomfortable with things that could make me feel sad. That's when I decided to use the stove for the first time. On my own, without my mom knowing. She always told me to stay away from the stove. I learned how to use it when I observed her cooking, and I asked her questions. My mom was always a great cook. She could cook anything. I liked to watch sometimes, wondering how food would transform.

I placed a pan on the stove. I turned on the gas and pressed on the lighter button that flickered till there was fire. It took me awhile to get the hang of which was supposed to come first. I got the bottle of cooking oil and I poured in about a tablespoon of it. It got smoky. I lowered the fire and rushed to find something to cook. I scanned the fridge. I found a bag of medium sized dried anchovies at the bottom. I counted three fillets and I quickly dropped them in the hot oil. I found a spatula and I stirred the anchovies around, as it cooked in what seemed like seconds. I turned off the stove and I got the anchovies out on a plate with the spatula. I tasted it and it was good. I successfully made fried anchovies. I got some water from the tap to sprinkle it in the pan. I watched it sizzle and smoke in different levels of intensity.

I repeated this entire process, I would say, at least ten times in a row. It appears I had nothing better to do. Somewhere in the middle of it, I felt stupid, but it felt addictive. I gradually increased the number of anchovies to five. I wanted to figure out how to cook perfectly without the sprinkling oil and the smoke. I tried to figure out how to fry without getting sprinkled with hot sizzling oil. My head was just a level higher than the stove, so the oil kept splattering on my face. It was scary. I kept my distance like my mom always told me to. I wondered why it kept happening and if there was a way for it to not be like that.

Then, I went to my mom and convinced her that I could fry. She didn't believe me at first, but she eventually asked me to make her a meal as no one was around to help her in bed. She explained how to make rice. It was my first time to. I made her plain rice with butter on it, and a fried egg. It all went well. She was very grateful and she was so happy. Then later on at eleven years old, I won a cooking competition. All the curiosity and silly experiments paid off in the end.

While cooking as a married woman, Khatijah started going to the kitchen to check what I was preparing. She kept hurrying downstairs only for the purpose of bothering my cooking. She tried to take over my cooking rudely, in her way. I wanted to have early dinner one night without Adam, because Adam wasn't going to be home until around midnight. He told me not to worry about dinner, so I decided to make something light and simple for myself.

I wanted to have breakfast food. All I wanted was to fry a simple sunny side up to have with toast. I prepared the egg, the oil, the bread, and I was looking for more bottles of seasonings. Khatijah hurried downstairs to meet me at that point.

"What are you making?" she asked, immediately as she entered the kitchen. She didn't even look at me. She was looking at the ingredients I prepared.

"Oh, I'm just gonna fry an egg," I said, with a slight smile. It was a very calm and peaceful day alone for me.

"Why don't you try it like this," she said. She quickly, and aggressively, got a saucer from the drawer. She added a little bit of water in it from the water dispenser. She placed it on the counter, then grabbed the egg and cracked it into the saucer. She took the bottle of oil I had prepared to use, and added what seemed like a little bit too much for frying a single egg. She was going really fast, as if she had a timer. Then she turned around and carefully popped it in the microwave behind her, and set it to thirty seconds.

It felt so rude, but I was still enjoying the silence I had in my mind. I was patient and curious enough to see what would happen. When we got her masterpiece out, I just politely laughed.

"It's okay," I said.

She looked at it with me, then she looked at me. She drained it and threw it out in the trash, then hurried back upstairs immediately. She continued trying to change my style of cooking, regularly.

"You should've used a bigger pot," she said to me. I was making Adam spaghetti carbonara, his favorite pasta.

"Oh, no, I wanna use this one," I said. I went back to stirring the carbonara sauce I made with extra mushrooms, chopped onions, cheese, and others. Adam was never picky with food, so I was able to add whatever I wanted.

"You should use a bigger pot," she insisted. I understood her, because it's very common to use a large pot for boiling pasta. But it really just depends on the cook.

"Oh, this is more energy saving," I answered her.

She looked at the pot. She shrugged and left the kitchen.

I pre-made popcorn chicken bites from scratch quite often, to deep fry and enjoy with Adam. Khatijah also gave us some 'keropok lekor', a Malaysian snack that was made of fish and flour, shaped like sausages, that was supposed to be fried. She didn't even like me frying either one. We always had to use her air fryer, only. The air fryer was good and healthy, but once in awhile we did want to enjoy some juicy, deep fried snacks. They would have been deep fried if we bought them from restaurants, anyway.

"Don't use so much oil," she said, when she saw me deep frying.

I thought I just didn't realize how much oil I poured in. The next time I did, I poured in less.

"Don't use so much oil," she said, again. "Just use half of that. And then flip it."

"Okay," I said. I agreed, because I didn't mind doing so. It's not a big deal to me.

Until the next time, she came in the kitchen before I started.

"You're deep frying again?"

"Yeah," I said.

"Here," she said. She poured in the oil for me. "Just use that much."

It wasn't even half of what I had the last time, at all. It was just a covered layer over the pan. She wanted me to deep fry using minimal oil, barely even dipping anything in it. It was impossible to let the popcorn chicken fry on its own, to cover every edge of it, and the insides, too. Popcorn chicken isn't even flat. Same thing with the keropok lekor. It wasn't considered deep frying at all, and it only consumed more of my time to fry them all evenly.

To make matters worse in the kitchen, all of a sudden, I couldn't find my groceries. Khatijah had relocated them randomly, with no notice or logical explanation at all. I wasted a lot of time with that. This continued to happen regularly. I usually had to search for my ingredients and asked her where they were. Not only did I lose my spiritual freedom, but I had suddenly lost the freedom of cooking, too.

9

CATS AND CRAP

There were always stray cats around the house, as there were many in the neighborhood. I've always been an animal lover. Even with cat allergies, I always loved taking care of them, however much that I could. It was during the day, sometime after breakfast. I got some of Jinan's food in a plastic, disposable container. I wanted to feed some to a mother cat and her kittens outside. Khatijah was right next to me in the kitchen, while I was in front of the sink, facing the window.

"What are you doing?" she asked, while working on something she got in a plastic bag, on the kitchen counter.

"Feeding the cats," I said, pointing to the cats in our view.

"No, don't feed them!" she stopped me.

"Why?" I asked her. I was worried.

"They're going to poo everywhere," she said.

"Really?"

"Yeah, they poo everywhere if you feed them."

She opened the back door that was just a few steps to our left, and pointed to most of the areas outside. The tiles, the cement, the wooden back porch.

"They'll poo all over here," she said.

"Really?" I was surprised. I didn't want that to happen either. I was sad that I couldn't feed them.

"Yeah," she said. "So don't feed them."

The very next day, I ordered flamed-grilled chicken delivery from a restaurant for us to have at home. She had some, then went to wash her hands and dishes in the kitchen.

"Feed the bones to the stray cats when you're done," she shouted from the kitchen.

"Okay," Adam and I said. I acted dumb, as if she never said what she said the day before.

She walked back to the dining table and stood in front of us.

"Just rinse the bones and feed them. Don't throw them away," she said, while pointing to the chicken Adam was having.

"Okay," we both said and nodded to her.

"It's not good to throw away food when we can feed them to animals. Ustad (an Islamic scholar) said that we must feed them. They need to be fed," she said.

"Okay," we said, and nodded while busy with our food.

It was odd to me. She acted like she was teaching us something new. But she clearly knew I wanted to feed the cats. She continued acting that way for the rest of the week, telling us to focus on feeding the cats. There wasn't any poo every time we fed them, though.

Khatijah rarely paid attention to Jinan. But when she knew that I was allergic to cats, she didn't like Jinan spending her time outside.

"Don't let her out!" she said.

She made us stop her from leaving the house, even though Jinan was used to the outdoors.

When Jinan was out, she said, "Don't let her out for too long." Even though it was just early in the day, and we knew how to take care of her as we always did.

When I let Jinan out while I rested comfortably in the room, she kindly knocked on the bedroom door.

"She wants to go in the room," she said.

She did this regularly. I wasn't sure if Jinan really wanted to be in the room, or if she just didn't want to be around Khatijah. Jinan normally sat in front of the door as close to the door as possible and looking up at me when I opened the door. Khatijah would be behind her. A lot of times when Khatijah came home and I had the bedroom door opened, Jinan ran to stay with me and cuddle up to me. Although Jinan was always such a baby with me anyway, her anxiety worried me.

It didn't really bother me what the arrangement was going to be, though. Jinan was clearly very attached to me, so I treated her like she was my own child. I just didn't want Jinan to be uncomfortable in any way and for me to be the reason for her discomfort.

However, before I got married to Adam, I needed to know if everything would be okay. Of course, as it was only logical to, I addressed my concerns of his cat one day.

"I have cat allergies, so it might be a problem," I said. "It's really really bad. I can sneeze the moment I step even one foot in the house, if it's not clean. And I can really be dying."

"Don't worry, she can be outside most of the time," he answered.

"But I don't want her to have to change her environment because of me. And even if she's outside a lot, I can still get affected by her dander in the house. It's the dander, not the cat," I said. "And I can't do the vacuuming myself 'cause that's when it affects me the worst," I added. Most vacuums have wind that blows out, which ends up blowing dander around. "The dander can fly everywhere."

"Don't worry, I'll vacuum every two weeks, okay? And if it's still not enough, you just let me know," he said.

I was so surprised. He sounded so hardworking and willing to do a lot for me without me even asking. I was happy with the answer, so I agreed that it would be good.

After about three months into the marriage, I eventually knew I had to do all of the cleaning myself. If I were willing to wait for him, it could go on longer than a month. I tried once, but it wasn't good for me. Obviously. I felt like I was deteriorating from the weakened immune system, and I had horrible skin breakouts and reactions for a long time. I also had symptoms of cold and flu just about every day, when the room wasn't vacuumed. It kept me in a cycle of sickness. It was very hard to deal with, considering I was fighting allergies and I was busy with uni assignments.

I kept being patient with Adam, though. For an entire year, I ended up spending on various supplements and medications, every month, using my own money. Healing myself from the allergies was a need. I was unwell most days for about two years, because of it. For two years, I was in a cycle of allergies and healing.

Eventually, and finally, Adam decided to invest in some bottles of supplements that he was introduced to, for me. It was initially for a business investment, but it didn't matter. I was very happy. I was excited about it and I took it every day. Then after a while, I suddenly got cured. Till today, I no longer have allergic reactions to cats the way I ever had it before in my life. Which made me glad that I had to experience all the allergies to begin with.

Then, Khatijah started saying that Jinan should be outside. If we cared about Jinan a lot, as we always did, this time around she started telling us, "She's just an animal!"

She habitually said that to us. It was offensive, considering how much we loved and cared for Jinan as our own child. It's a completely normal love, for people with pets. We obviously always knew that Jinan's a cat, and that cats are animals. Her cat problems seemed to be worse than the cat allergies I had. All this happened throughout the span of two years. (Until later on in our third year, I got myself my own kitten, and she said she wanted one too.)

Meanwhile, early in the marriage, I learned that not only did Khatijah not understand love for animals, but perhaps love for family, too. None of the disrespectful things she did before spoke as loud as what I was blessed to be aware of, one day.

It was after a religious class that Khatijah hosted at her house. It was still a bright day, in the afternoon. We just had our refreshments. Adam and I were standing outside the house on the driveway, on our own. Adam was being sweet, holding me, and talking to me. We tend to be that way during events, and I especially loved making him look good. It was one of the things I always loved for my man.

All of a sudden, one of Adam's first cousins once-removed, Mak Rubi, who is Khatijah's cousin, came to interrupt us. In between us, she stood facing the house, to my right. We smiled and greeted her kindly as we did with others. She wanted to talk to us.

"Adam, why don't you spend some time with your mom?" she asked Adam.

I nodded in agreement while looking at Adam.

I said, "Yeah, go out and spend time with her."

Although he was already seeing and talking to her everyday at home, and going for regular breakfasts with her. Adam was quiet about it, and calm. He was mostly smiling, as he usually did with people. He was listening. I didn't really know what Mak Rubi was on about. But it was still a good thing for him to spend time with his mother.

Then she looked at me and said, "You, why don't you stay away for a while. Stay somewhere else." She moved her arms out to point to the air behind her, swinging it as if showing me where to go. "Maybe a few months... at least six months... or something. Let Adam's mom get used to the marriage first... It's something so new for her. I feel bad seeing her like this. It's not easy for her," she said, and looked at Khatijah. I was quite appalled by what she was saying to me. I realized she had no shame at all, acting rather insolent. I was always kind to her. I was calm, but I didn't understand why she was saying that to me.

Through the sliding door, the three of us was looking at Khatijah, who was organizing the dining table with the other women. She was facing us, but she had her face down at the time, looking rather sad as Mak Rubi was portraying.

"I pity her," she continued. "It's sad seeing her like this, you know... She's sad. Let her get used to it first. The marriage is still so new for her..."

Mak Rubi was looking at both of us while continuing her failed persuasion. Adam was just listening, but not really listening to her, as he told me later on.

"Oh, no! I've never stopped Adam from spending time with

his mom, you know?" I had one hand out in front of me, slightly moving it back and forth with my fingers spread out, as if calming her futility down. "I always tell him to," I said, making it clear of what it's been like.

I was always worried about both Adam's and Khatijah's well-beings. They were the most important people to me since marriage. Besides, if Adam and I ever wanted to be separated while married, it wouldn't make sense for me to stay away in order for Khatijah to 'get used to the marriage'. It also wouldn't make sense that Adam was so passionate to marry me, but yet end up not living with me. I thought she could have been assuming that I was clingy or possessive, which I have never been. In fact, if I were to ask Adam when he would be back home by, or where he was, a few times he would ask me, "Why don't you just say that you miss me?" I do have my romantic moments, obviously. I have told him that I missed him as well, but I'm generally more practical. I express my love through actions rather than easy words. I found myself too busy a lot of times, too, keeping myself occupied with a lot of work and studies. I needed to get the important things done and out of the way first.

Mak Rubi became hesitant and stuttering her words, not able to look at me in the eye. She was looking at Khatijah's direction while Adam and I watched her.

"Oh. No. No..." she said, looking deep and distracted in her thoughts. "She didn't say anything about you." She pointed at me while shaking her head, still looking at Khatijah. "Yeah, nothing about you."

That's when it was clear to me. That regardless of whether Mak Rubi was telling the truth or not about Khatijah not saying anything about me, Khatijah still did say something to her. Mak Rubi has made it clear that she got such ideas from Khatijah. It was shocking.

Every single day, and throughout the day, Khatijah was communicating with Adam. Whether she would call him, or message him continuously. Just about every single time Adam was spending time with me, she demanded to be answered and to chat with him. I have always trusted her unconditionally from the beginning, as she was my mother-in-law. I allowed her to be a part of my private life, and I was only ever open and compromising with her. I took care of her son and was always concerned with his well-being. I sacrificed a lot of myself to keep him happy and anything he would ask of me. In return, she was playing around a game of manipulation against me.

10

FOREIGN LOVE

It was June, 2014. Around two months before, about the second month of our marriage, Khatijah scheduled a flight to London for us to visit Adam's dad's side of the family as newlyweds. She wanted to bring us to London, and then we were to go to Paris afterwards, because she had some extra airline miles to use on us. However, I wasn't even aware that it was scheduled, and that it was also during my thesis. We had just gotten married, too. I was shocked that I didn't know about it, so I told Adam to postpone it.

We were in our bedroom, when he was making me agree to book the ticket on another day as soon as possible.

"Just choose a day, baby, any day," he said, lying next to me, facing me with his arms supporting his weight. I could tell he was pressured to make me go.

"I don't know yet, I need some time to think about it," I sulked.

"Let's just get it over with, baby," Adam said, with a worried look over me, holding my arms while facing me.

For a few seconds, I didn't respond to him. I was thinking, and he was waiting for me to think.

All of a sudden, before it could even get to five seconds, Khatijah suddenly stormed in the room out of nowhere and started begging me. It startled me. I was lying down, practically naked through my sheer night slip, so I quickly grabbed the blanket to cover myself with it. I don't even know what to say about that. She had no courtesy to knock on the door, or even bang on it like she she should have loved to do. She didn't notify us in any way at all.

Khatijah just walked right in to beg me, with her desperate, whining expression, slightly shaking dramatically. She bent down to have her face about a foot away from my face.

She said, "Just go...! Don't worry, just go!" while putting her hands slightly on the bed.

If I had some time to respond, it would've been a silent awkward moment with just my eyes moving. I didn't understand where all the drama was coming from. All it was to me was that I was going through some minor problems with my husband in our bedroom. It was a private thing.

She continued begging me, telling me to go. I had my hands up to my neck holding the blanket, watching her with no expressions. My head was slightly pulled back because she was too close. It was so rude to me, I just wanted her out of the room. But I watched her fatuous performance. I was very uncomfortable. She left once she was done, leaving me and Adam to continue with what we were already up to from before she invaded our privacy. That was also when I learned that Khatijah could hear everything we talked about from outside the room, despite her hearing problems. She liked to pick and choose what she could hear, and what she couldn't hear. Adam was quiet about the whole thing and acted like it was normal. He tried to make me believe it was, by acting like as if nothing happened. Maybe he was too embarrassed to admit his mom was strange. Or maybe he did think it was normal, however odd that would be.

It was still difficult to schedule the tickets at first, because of my thesis. However, Adam was persistent in making me agree to a date as soon as possible, so I eventually held back a semester for it. I thought it wasn't the best timing. But I went for it anyway.

Uncle Ralph's was a two-storey suburban house in the corner with spacious backyard. The neighborhood, and the exterior red bricks of the house, reminded me of the suburbs in Texas. The cooling, fresh air outside, and the smell of trees through the clean wind felt like Texas during spring. Their carpeted and wooden interior reminded me of childhood. Their all white, bare window frames welcoming the sun, facing their private outdoors, reminded me of the green and brightness I had at home in Texas, too. We had large, white window frames showing off our spacious green backyard and playground. It reminded me so much of a life I once had. I felt a stimulating, familiar connection, and I immediately loved being there.

I had already met Uncle Ralph and Aunt Laura on our wedding day and I loved them both, since. They were my favorite in-laws. They were always lighthearted and they got along with me the best. Khatijah, on the other hand, seemed so grumpy by how well I was getting along with them. During meals, she kept rolling her eyes and looking at me in a mean, jealous way from the corner of her eyes so much. Even when I was right in front of her. And even when Aunt Laura, who was right next to her, was talking to her. I almost thought her eyes were just going to stay that way. It was disturbing, and very upsetting, but it didn't stop me from having fun with my favorite relatives. Nor did it stop me from being patient and kind to Khatijah. There was no way I would hold back my studies for some bad family time, especially after travelling for hours and getting a little flu from the flight, too.

I was already used to Khatijah doing that to me daily back in Malaysia, obviously. I just couldn't believe she couldn't control herself at all, around my paternal in-laws. Her jealousy was raging even worse there. Maybe it was difficult for her to manipulate Uncle Ralph and Aunt Laura the way she was able to with her side of the family and friends. With Adam's dad's side of the family, she was a clear-cut hater unable to contain herself.

Then, one morning after breakfast, I had a heart-to-heart talk with Aunt Laura, who officially became the best person in the family to me. It felt so refreshing and welcoming. She's a few decades older than me, but she was so sharp that it felt like I was just talking to a woman in her thirties. We talked about quite a lot of things. She was so open-minded, unbiased, and direct. She helped me more than any of the other relatives I had ever talked to.

Everyone else was occupied with other things. Khatijah was busy fixing her hearing aid in her room. It suddenly started attacking her with a high pitch ringing sound during breakfast that wouldn't stop. And yes, while she was busy giving me the galling looks.

Finally, it was the only time I had alone with Aunt Laura. I followed her around the kitchen as I watched her put some dishes away, talking to me. The soft sunlight was reflecting on her wavy, golden blonde hair, distracting me from what could be inside the cupboards. We stopped by the oven, and she gave me some unexpected advice.

"We can see Khatijah trying to control you. It's very obvious," she said, serious and concerned. I was so surprised, but I was so relieved. Finally, there were some humans that I've been blessed to be in contact with, who were kind enough to acknowledge the reality of my situation. I was always on my own when it was Khatijah's side of the family.

"You noticed?" I asked, with my eyes wide, staring into her big, hypnotic blue eyes that were staring into mine just the same. In that moment, I didn't see anything else around me. She caught my complete attention. I was so focused, it was almost like a dream, how everything else got blurry.

"Oh yes, it's very obvious. You don't have to tell us," she said, nodding at me with her eyes wide. I finally saw the rest of her.

I was unsure if I should tell Aunt Laura anything about it, because Khatijah was my mother-in-law after all. I couldn't respond to her. I was too indecisive.

"You should stand up for yourself. Just because she's your mother-in-law, doesn't mean you have to accept them," she said. I didn't know how she could read me so well. I was happy and accepting with Khatijah. I was acting the same way with Khatijah's side of the family too, but none of them ever noticed anything. "You don't have to allow it," Aunt Laura said. She was very serious about it. She seemed so experienced. "Some things are not right and they shouldn't be accepted, regardless of who they are to you," she made it clear for me to understand. She felt more like a mother to me than Khatijah ever was.

I knew she was right. I've always known that. But somehow, I've only kept choosing to be patient. I felt better knowing that I wasn't the only one aware of Khatijah's true nature. And that it also wasn't a bad thing at all that I was aware of it. And more importantly, that it was very real. I just never had any support for what I was already aware of. It felt like Aunt Laura was the first perceptive person I've talked to in a long time.

"Yeah, I know…" I said, while looking around us in distraction. I was still indecisive. I was hoping no one could hear us, too. I looked at her again and waited.

"You have your rights. You don't have to do everything she tells you to," she repeated herself. "What does Adam think about this?"

I didn't want to tell her what Adam has been like, either. I didn't know what to say.

"Adam wants to be religious," I said, quite randomly. I didn't know if she would be able to get a hint of what I meant. Adam was always very good at containing himself around certain people.

"Good! I wouldn't want anything less for him," she said with sincerity. Her face was serious. She looked out the window to where Adam was, outside with Uncle Ralph. I watched her blue eyes shining from the soft sunlight. I wanted to know that perspective. What was her perspective of Adam? What are her memories? Then she revealed, "Khatijah would never be covered up around Ralph before you," she pointed downwards to the floor, shaking it for emphasis of the present time. I looked at her pointing hand, then back at her. She was shaking her head at the same time.

"She wouldn't cover herself up?" I asked, surprised.

"No!" she answered, in a higher pitch, short and detached. She shook her head and rolled her eyes slightly to the side to recall. "She was here last year, too."

I took a moment to process that.

"Last… year…?" I asked to confirm.

"Yeah!" she said in a higher pitch, short and detached again, absolutely sure. "She would just remove it every time we were home. Ralph would see her uncovered," she said, while making gestures of removing a headscarf with her hands.

The previous year was just about the time Khatijah met me. She was already supposedly all 'Sunnah', following the Prophet's way, at the time. She was supposed to be all holy for years, before ever meeting me. She held the reputation of an old religious woman, and she was very active with the Sunnah organization for a while, too.

Clearly, Uncle Ralph isn't blood related to Khatijah, which means that she was also able to marry him. That also means if she was really a religious woman who is covered up, she wouldn't be exposing herself to him whenever she wanted to. It shocked me, considering it was also around the time I was invited to the house for one of her religious classes that she was hosting.

Things just got dodgier with Khatijah than it already ever was.

According to Adam, Khatijah only started covering up after he asked her, "Why don't you wear the headscarf?" He was just a little boy seeing all the women around him in headscarves. So she decided to.

Since Adam's father died as a Catholic when he was a toddler, according to Islam, the marriage gets annulled. If Adam's father never became Muslim again within a certain period, which he didn't get to, the marriage immediately gets declared invalid. Adam's father never got to become Muslim again, because he died as a Catholic, which also made Khatijah even more of a stranger to the family, according to Islam. Uncle Ralph wasn't even her brother-in-law.

I also noticed that both Adam and his mom weren't how they normally would be. Adam was a lot quieter, as if waiting for his mom to do what she had to do, but he was always decent with them regardless. From Adam's energy and body language, it was always as if he was holding back on a lot of things he wished he could say.

I never questioned it, though, because I knew Khatijah was in a financial muddle with Uncle Ralph and Aunt Laura. I figured that's why it felt a little odd. Khatijah claimed that Aunt Laura and Uncle Ralph have her money that was never given to her. She said that Adam's paternal grandfather was supposed to give her a lot of his money, but instead, Uncle Ralph and Aunt Laura were still keeping it from her, and have spent a lot of it on their own home and luxury.

It's hard for me to believe Uncle Ralph and Aunt Laura would do that. I highly doubt Khatijah ever had rights to the money, either. It's quite creepy, to me, considering she liked to visit and stay with them in their house every year.

When we got to Paris, Adam was suddenly being outrageously rude almost all the time. He was being that way when we were staying at the hotel in London, too. We stayed at a hotel for a few days before going to Uncle Ralph's. We went for long walks on our own without Khatijah. Every time we had minor disagreements such as whether we should walk or take a cab back home, he left me stranded all alone. It was so obnoxious, and senseless, considering it's not all the time that we could be romantic in Europe. I couldn't believe how we were spending our time. If I tried to catch up to him, or tell him to stop, he would ignore me. He would continue walking faster and disappear. I didn't have data there, so I couldn't use my phone to contact him at all.

Same thing happened when he would abandon me in Paris. I wasn't scared of being alone. But I admit being in a foreign country all alone like that, not knowing if he was coming back to find me, or expect me to go back to the hotel myself, was quite worrying for me. I was never sure if it was the right time to find a ride back, because I was worried about him. I thought, if there's no way for me to contact him, then how do I know that he's fine? What if something happens to him? These were my thoughts every time it happened. He was always nowhere to be seen, and I was left alone in the dark cold nights.

I was disappointed with him, but I never cried. I've never really been the emotional type. I do cry, but just not that easy to, and especially not in public. I just remained calm and enjoyed whatever was around me, peacefully, while wondering why he is the way he is, until he would eventually come back to find me. If I ever had to go back to the hotel room on my own, neither Adam nor Khatijah would ask me where I was or what happened to me. They would act indifferent, and I had to act like everything was just fine, too.

Luckily, everyone I met in Paris kept thinking that I was French. They were very surprised to hear that I'm not. I was able to socialize quite a lot with both men and women who randomly came up to me, whether Adam left me around some busy bars, or the dark and silent parts of town. I was quite enjoying the fascination I had for the locals, and them, me. I never quite understood why Malaysians tend to say they hate Paris. I loved it there. They treated me so much better.

I felt God accompanying me the whole time, cheering me up through other people. One of the guys that came up to me was very expressive with his interest in me. He sure seemed a lot sweeter than what I was going through. I felt like I was being tested with temptations. It reminded me of a time Adam left me at a cafe next door to our place in Malaysia. I was sad but I was calm. I left the cafe to go home on my own. The next thing I knew, a cute foreigner came running after me to the parking lot and asked me if I was single.

I knew I didn't have to freak out when Adam treated me like shit. I always had a strong feeling I would be cheered up after. Similarly, in London and Paris, it was through such faith that I was able to persevere. It amused me how I was still approachable even with Muslimah wear. They were so open minded. I had fun.

Also one of those nights, Adam left me alone by a big river. It was dark, and it was quiet. There were always a few cars driving around the spacious road next to it, and sometimes I felt a little worried that there could be criminals or stalkers watching me. (I was stalked in Malaysia a few times all the way to my house before.) Only one woman passed me by the river, and she talked to me. She was also surprised that I wasn't French, and it made me laugh. I was alone the rest of the time. The entire long sidewalk I was on was probably empty. It was a beautiful night scenery, though. I imagined a painting of it.

Adam always came back to find me after a while, if we were far from the hotel. And so he eventually came back. It was freezing cold. Then he walked fast ahead of me to guide me to a cafe. I didn't even know we were going to a cafe. He didn't even tell me. We had hot drinks there to warm up. I was still fine with him. I was still just calm.

We left the cafe and took a cab back to the hotel. It seemed as if the cab driver saw what happened to me before picking us up. As if he knew I was stranded for a period of time. He was young like us. Very attractive. He was so confident and talkative. He sounded so sexy with his French accent and boyish nature. I felt an aura from him, like he was helping us in a way. He talked about how he's Muslim too, and that he was making a living and taking care of his wife. That it's not easy, but he's still focused on his responsibilities. I was speechless by what I was feeling, I couldn't talk. I couldn't even look at him. I was quite embarrassed. It was so intense. I felt blessed to have a man speak some sense to Adam. I didn't want Adam to be upset about it. He was talking too, but not as much. When we got out of the cab, he drove away very slowly. It was as if he was making sure we were okay. I remember him sometimes. I remember the effort he's left for my fucked up marriage in such a short time.

For our last dinner in Paris, we chose a restaurant at the corner of the block of our hotel. It just so happens I met all the workers there before, too. They were very happy to see me and we laughed together. We had a connection. They knew I was the naughty girl on my own at night, walking around the silent alleys. I waved at them as the hostess ushered us to our table. It was funny. I never told them a single thing about what I was going through. They had no idea.

The hostess was so beautiful. Average height and curvy. She had medium, soft, fine curly light brown hair, and blue eyes. When I first met her, she was instantly a long lost best friend. So much that I still miss her till this day. We hugged. When Adam and Khatijah saw the connection we had, Adam was pleased about it. Khatijah, though, could barely talk during dinner. She barely ate her food, then she excused herself to go back to the hotel room.

It's amazing to me how the British and the French were able to sense something wrong with my marriage so easily, and they were very quick to help me. My marriage was strange to me, too. Unfortunately, there was still no way for me to change that. I still had no idea what was really happening. I didn't know why everything was so messed up. It was absolutely, completely, only Adam's way, Khatijah's way, or no way at all. *At all.*

11

FEAR PLAY

Adam was unhappy with me. We had an argument on the phone. I was on the bed, working on my laptop and multitasking, when he came home. I talked to him while working. He grabbed my Macbook Pro and threw it on the floor. I couldn't believe what I was seeing, so much that I didn't think he really wanted to break it.

He threw my previous laptop before, too. A Sony Vaio. I really liked the shiny red cover it had. He broke it by pushing it off my bed aggressively. When I found that it was broken, he tried his best to persistently persuade me that it was always broken that way. But it had new rattling sounds and vibrations, sudden distorted screen, and everything else that wasn't functioning as well as it should have. It was still serving me well before that, as far as I knew. I wasn't able to use it without it shutting down on me every few minutes anymore, either.

But he kept picking up my Macbook and slamming it to the floor. Pieces of the laptop flew around. This time I was sure he wasn't going to deny breaking it. He seemed to be enjoying the adrenaline from being able to. I kept myself calm, not wanting to make the situation any worse. I was on the edge of the bed in the corner by then, leaning against the headboard. He picked up the chunk of metal that was once a laptop and threw it at me. I blocked myself against it with my arms and it gave me several deep cuts.

He grabbed my Sony Cybershot camera that was on the computer table, and he threw it at me. I blocked it and it fell to the floor with broken pieces of it scattered. It was my favorite camera because it was pink and it was touch screen. It also had a quick sliding cover to turn it on and off. It was a gift from my mom that I wanted to keep for a long time. It was working so well for years.

He grabbed an old Nokia phone of mine from the computer table, too, and he threw it at me like baseball. The same thing happened to it. I blocked it, then pieces of it broke as it touched the floor. I was using that phone for years as an extra phone, in cases of emergency, and for outdoor activities.

Adam left the room.

My heart was beating fast, but I didn't have much reaction to it. I was just wondering why he's so screwed up. I picked up all the broken pieces of gadgets I could find around me, and placed them on the bed in front of me. I tried putting them together. They were all completely broken.

The Macbook was completely destroyed, all over. In it I had my thesis research, my waffle catering website materials that I was working on with my developer, and a lot of other important documents that I had been working on every day. I made a loss because I had already paid my developer for an entire year, but I was then unable to continue with him, due to the unexpected lack of content.

As with everything else of mine that was destroyed in the house, I never got compensated. I was bitter about my Macbook, though. I needed it to continue working and it was unfair that he made me lose so much. He took me to some shops to ask them if they could fix it, but it felt like a joke. The Macbook looked like a demonic creature squatted over it, peeled its' metal layers with its' crooked teeth, to search for an actual apple inside. I mean, how could a Macbook ever end up looking that, even if it got run over by a car? No shop, not even the best who were used to fixing gadgets in secret for VIPs, were able to fix it. I couldn't believe all the work I had done night and day, were all gone.

It wasn't easy for me to get my Macbook replaced. He kept stalling, as if it didn't matter. I had so much work to do, and even more then, after the damages. I was oppressed at home, unable to do any work, and suddenly unable to work on my laptop quietly in the bedroom, too.

After a week went by of waiting, I decided to get Adam to understand how it feels. I left a scratch on his PC screen. It was a small diagonal scratch at the corner. It didn't even block his view. It wouldn't even affect his work.

"Look," I said to him, and pointed to the scratch. He just got home. "That's for all the times you broke my things."

He was so devastated.

"What did you do!!!" he was so shocked about it like it was the end of the world. How typical.

I told him, "At least it's still working, unlike everything of mine that's suddenly gone now."

He didn't understand it at all. "You're getting me a new one," he said.

"No I'm not? Why should I?" I asked him. "All my things are still gone."

"You're getting me a new one now," he said.

"Nope, not unless you get me a new Macbook," I said.

"I can't get it now, I told you I need more time," he said.

"How much longer?" I asked.

"I don't know," he answered, looking distracted in thoughts.

"Then you shoulda thought of that before you broke everything," I said, and watched him.

"I already told you I'm getting you a new one!" he said in frustration.

"No you're not...?" I called bluff.

"I am getting you a new one!" he insisted.

"When? Can you get it today?" I quickly asked.

"No. I don't know yet," he answered.

"Then I don't know if I can get you the new screen," I said.

"Give me till this weekend," he said.

"You promise?" I asked. "You promise you're getting me the new Macbook this weekend?"

"Promise."

I immediately went out to the shop with him to buy the new screen. He kept his promise with the Macbook at the end of the week, too.

Only being rational, though, I still wanted a divorce. I was needing it. I needed to know if it was possible to mutually divorce, in peace. I was too bothered by how horrible we were together. If I was so horrible that he would abuse me and damage my things, then surely he wouldn't mind letting me go for some peace of mind for himself, too. Or so I thought.

About a month from the last tantrum, I tried having the talk. He bought me fried rice for lunch, and placed it on the bed. It was in a Styrofoam container.

"Thank you!" I said to him.

"You're welcome," he responded, as he headed calmly for the door. I'm not sure where he was going, though.

"Um, we need to talk," I said. I thought it was the best time to, seeing how he was calm.

He stopped and looked at me. He was right in front of me.

With no hesitation, I asked, "What do you think about a mutual divorce?"

He seemed so uneasy. He was looking around, distracted, breathing heavily in anxiety.

"Everything will be okay. We can still be friends. We were better as friends, anyway."

I couldn't help it. I was serious. I needed to know and it just needed to be done.

Then came another one. He pushed me down to the bed and started swinging his fist at me.

"You say the D word one more time!!" he yelled with passion as he continued swinging at me.

As he got off me to stand up, I immediately grabbed the fried rice on the bed and swung it on his head. The rice went everywhere.

He came towards me instantly and tried to grab me.

I grabbed both his arms before he could, and he resisted. I hit his arms and felt like it hurt me more than it hurt him. I knew it wasn't the same thing when I hit him. I had no muscles or fat anywhere on my arms.

By the time he was done with me, my new satin comforter that I had bought with my own savings, was covered with rice. It was so gross. That was my fault.

He grabbed the comforter in a ball and went downstairs with it. He left me to heal in the room as usual. I thought he went to put it in the washer. Two days later, I opened the dryer and it wasn't in there. I double checked the outside, in front, and at the back, to be sure that I didn't miss it. I couldn't find it anywhere.

I went to him sitting in front of the computer and asked, "Where's the comforter?"

"I threw it away," he said. He looked at me calmly with his eyes telling me he was surprised I didn't know.

I couldn't believe he did that. It was new and it cost me more than a thousand ringgit. I was so upset. I sat down and rationalized my feelings for the comforter. I didn't get angry.

"Can you get a new comforter?" I asked him calmly.

"Okay," he said, sounding enthusiastic.

A few days later, he replaced it with a rough cotton quilt that looked like it was from the local street market. It was uncomfortable and it hurt my sensitive skin. It collected a lot of cat fur, too. I didn't like it at all. We ended up donating it.

There seemed to be a routine of abusing me after every time I was healed and able to feel 'normal' again. I couldn't see this at the time. Sometimes it was a lot more tolerable; sometimes near-death horrifying. I always believed that he would stop, or that he would really change, as he would say. This is because before marrying him, I never thought he would be this way at all. I could never see it. I kept thinking there was something wrong somewhere in the marriage, or somewhere in his life. I kept thinking I had to fix something. But there was nothing.

I drove to the Syariah court twice before, but got too nervous to enter. I didn't know what I would say. I didn't know how they would entertain me, if they would at all. Women unable to get divorced from their screwed up husbands have been a big issue in the Muslim community. It happened to one of my friends, too. I asked Adam for a divorce after every abuse. Sometimes I acted like I was allowed to divorce him and say, "I divorce you". But unfortunately, Syariah law doesn't work like that. But Adam still cried so easily after every divorce requests and attempts.

I never understood why, and how, he could harm me and love me at the same time. Growing up in Texas, a physical fight ends it all. If anyone had problems, there will most definitely be confrontation, and if a fight takes place, it's just a common way to end everything. And then it's time to move on. No guy fights with a girl, though. That's just immediately abuse. It's terribly unfair, and it just makes him a pussy. Only pussies fight with girls.

Adam begged and bawled his eyes out crying for me, every single time. How does anyone cry so much like that? A lot of times he got desperate enough to threaten suicide.

It was then a newfound routine to threaten me with suicide, then run out of the house, making me worried that I would be responsible for his death. I've known very emotional men in the past, but never to the extent of all that Adam had done. He would try to emotionally manipulate me, and I fell for it a few times at the beginning. Only because he was my husband, though, that I allowed myself to still care. He would be so persistent that I would eventually reach the point where I would feel too sorry for him and just comfort him. I felt responsible for him and his life.

Throughout the three years of being married to him, the threats would go on anytime from just a few minutes, then gradually increasing up to ten hours throughout the day, till night time. Or even from night time, till the next morning, keeping me awake from sleep until I would pass out when the sun comes out. A few times, I thought of calling the cops to do a search for me so I could sleep, but I thought I would have to wait for a while. It would have been too odd for me to call the cops asking to look for my husband. I think they would've just told me to wait, too.

Eventually, I had a feeling Adam would sleep in the car because he would come home with enough energy for the day. Then true enough, I found him in his car sometimes, sleeping. Twice, he surprised me with a mark on his upper forehead. They were most likely from banging his head on the steering wheel, as he did before a couple of times in front of me. Maybe he wanted attention. Maybe he wanted me to feel sympathy because he knows I'm sympathetic. Or maybe he was just plain nuts, period. But I didn't think that. I couldn't think that.

Adam was never embarrassed with his forehead marks.

"What if people see that? You should wear your cap," I suggested.

"They won't," he said, so sure.

"But it's so obvious," I said. I kept looking at the mark. It was small, but it was so red and up high on his forehead, in the middle. It was still very obvious.

"No, no one would care," he said.

I felt suspicious. Was he acting dumb? Did he just want attention from people?

Then he came home later that night from hanging out with his friends, and told me that someone just made a joke about it. I thought it was odd that no one really cared enough to find out. He seemed to be happy that people noticed, though. He had a calm smile about it.

I used to think he would run his car over a lamp post or purposely get in a car accident to kill himself. I was so worried. But I finally got to confirm that one day when he tried to win my love back after beating me. We were on the phone.

"I'm going to kill myself," he said.

"Okay… and how are you going to do that?" I asked.

"With the air conditioner," he answered.

"The air conditioner?" I asked again to be sure.

"I'll sleep in the car and get intoxicated by it," he said.

"What a joke," I said. "Only babies die in the car like that."

"Whatever," he said.

When he realized I stopped caring about his suicide threats, they soon decreased. He never stopped it entirely, but the threats became a lot easier to tolerate with my sarcastic responses.

That wasn't the only way he tried to control me with fear. He made me believe that no other man would treat me better. He had just finished letting out his frustrations on me again. He sat on a two-seater vintage rattan sofa right outside our bedroom. Next to it a wide, white, open shelving for files. Directly in front of him a blue, metal coffee table with wheels. On it some scattered books and remote controls. He was facing the TV, but the TV wasn't on. He sat there, thinking. I came to unravel his problems.

"I'm sure none of your friends would do the same to their wives," I said, as I moved in carefully to sit next to him. I watched the side of his face. I felt so bad for him. Why was he so messed up?

"You don't know them. They cheat on their wives," he said, as usual, annoyed with how I had the tendency to think highly of others.

"They cheat on their wives? As their husbands? They cheated, in the marriage?" I asked him, highly doubting it was true. He has told me about them cheating before, and I knew which ones specifically, but I never thought they would cheat their marriages, too.

"What do you think?" he asked me. He had his head turned slightly to look at me from the side.

"I don't think they do," I said. I was imagining it. It could actually be possible, though. But I couldn't be sure.

"The ones with money cheat on their bitch wives," he said. I didn't sense any deception in his tone. I scanned around in my imagination of them.

"Their wives are bitches?" I asked. He told me this before, too. I was secretly quite amused by his blunt answer. It's horrible. But right then, I wanted to know more.

"Their wives are materialistic corporate slaves and they backstab them all the time," he told me.

My mouth was opened, and I was speechless. At the same time, I held in a childish laugh. He sounded so serious with his hate for the nine-to-five kind of people. He always hated them.

After a long pause, I asked him, "How do you know they backstab them all the time?"

He answered, "They even have a group chat together to gossip and talk shit."

He sounded annoyed that I couldn't trust what he was saying from the beginning.

"How do you know they have a group chat to gossip and talk shit?" I asked.

"They're all aware of it," he answered me, annoyed. "They all chase after their selfish desires."

This was when I thought this was the reality of the Muslim community. This was the reality of my life. I was surrounded by people who don't seem to give the slightest care about life and love. It was hard for me to absorb. What's real anymore?

My parents had strong, beautiful love. I was exposed to idealistic love and marriage in the media as a child, through fairy tales, and growing up with the American dream. Boyfriends were always romantic, and I was a hopeless romantic, too. Love, as I was growing up, was always beautiful. A love relationship should be something to be proud of and to show off.

It's what I continued on believing, until what Adam was poisoning me with since the beginning of marriage. His culture. His friends. His world. It was all too much for me to deal with. Too many people take marriage for granted.

"Okay then, I'm sure none of your friends with no money would do the same to their wives," I said.

"They're still materialistic. They buy things they can't afford all the time. And they have to rely on borrowing from me," he said.

Everyone around him was doomed, I thought.

"Well, none of my ex-boyfriends would ever treat me as bad as you have," I said.

"Go ahead with them then," he said.

"Okay! Sure! I almost married them anyway," I answered immediately. I actually didn't mind it. Any guy at all would be a relief from the life I was in.

He looked down calmly in thoughts.

"Yeah... I should've married Romeo," I said.

"Yeah, go ahead with him. You said so yourself, he cheated on you," Adam quickly reminded me.

"Yeah, he did, he was drunk," I recalled.

"So that makes it okay?" he asked.

"No," I said, with hidden resentment. "But it's a lot better than getting abused. I would be able to accept it more."

He shook his head with disbelief in response.

I felt misunderstood. Romeo drunk kissed a girl and regretted it. Adam regularly and soberly abused me and never repented. I also stopped believing in the 'boyfriend girlfriend' relationship since then, anyway. Who can say anything is wrong at all when you're not legally wedded to each other?

However, I still felt guilty for bringing up an ex-boyfriend. I had only brought it up for Adam to understand what it means to love without all the chaos. And I told him this, when he was better again.

"I just needed you to understand that it's not normal to abuse whenever you want to. And it's especially not right to hurt your wife," I said, while comforting him.

We were driving back home after lunch that same week, around the neighborhood shop lot. It was a nice, fresh day out with him. It was a beautiful day. Not too bright, with just enough sun, enough wind, and with just the right temperature.

"Pervert. Pervert. Pervert," he said, while pointing around to random men.

I knew he was being childish. I felt so uncomfortable. He did this before, a lot of times. My abdomen felt uneasy, as if it was holding back anger. I knew I had no voice against him, as he would always hush off my opposing views.

"Umm… What are you doing?" I asked him.

"Beardless men are all perverts," he told me. "Pervert, pervert, pervert," he continued.

"No they're not…" I said.

"No, really, they're perverts. The Prophet hated them," he taught me.

"He loved everyone," I said. I could never believe the Prophet hated anyone. I believe he accepted so much abuse from people till he eventually had to fight through war. And that was it. The only people he seemingly 'hated', were people who were persistently asking for it.

"No, he wouldn't even look at them," he said.

I got so confused already. He seemed so sure.

"You used to be beardless. So you used to be a pervert," I made my deductions and waited for his answer.

He had no answer.

"Aww! He looks like such a good husband," I said, seeing a man so focused on helping his wife and baby.

"That's what you think," he said.

There's truth in that, because that's what everyone was thinking about Adam, weren't they? Wasn't he such a good husband for me? There were no other good men left. I thought Adam was the good one. He was supposed to be the good one amongst the others. The religious one. The one with morals.

12

EVERY GIRLS' DREAM

It was August, 2014. After London and Paris, we started planning our wedding reception. I invited everyone I was still in touch with. It was already planned during the engagement that we would only celebrate the marriage much later. We were supposed to let Khatijah plan everything for the reception, without us knowing anything. We weren't able to accept or reject any ideas, either. All that we could take part in was the choosing of my dress with the options given, and the preparing of door gifts.

Adam and I planned to find something new to wear for the occasion. For me, we went for a budget dress that was not paid by Adam, but Khatijah, for some reason. I didn't want to ask for anything better than the options I was given, because it wasn't even from Adam. After we all agreed to a soft yellow dress for me, Adam changed his mind and wanted to re-use what he wore for our wedding day. I didn't think it would look very nice, but he didn't care. I confronted him about it when we were in our bedroom.

I asked him, "Are you sure we're ready?"

I took the dress from the cupboard and held it against my body, looking at it.

"Yes, don't worry about it," he said, without looking. I trusted that he was sure about it, but he was occupied with something else when he answered.

"Are you sure? I don't know… It doesn't seem right anymore," I said.

"It's fine," he said.

"But, are you sure the dress looks nice? Maybe I should wear something else, something lighter," I suggested. "Or I can pay your mom back, and buy a different dress. A white one, to match yours more."

"There's nothing wrong with the dress," he answered, with a lack of energy and attention. He hated the conversation.

He always hated it when I talked about clothes. We were out once and I asked him about my headscarf. I kept repeating myself because he didn't bother to actually look at it at all. He still answered me, but it felt so insincere. After a few times of repeating myself, he surprised me with a sudden burst of anger and blurted out in Malay, which I found amusing. It was the first time anyone got so angry with me to the point of blurting in another language. He was always used to speaking English with me. I never experienced that before. All I did was smile back and burst out laughing a little when it happened, because I didn't think it was that bad.

"Baby, I'm so nervous. I'm not ready," I said.

He ignored me. I was so upset with his lack of response and understanding that I eventually said, "I don't think I want the reception anymore."

Then he finally answered me.

"Just do it!!!" he held on to his shout. He pushed me to the bed and immediately started shaking his entire body against me. I was blocking myself and trying to fight back at the same time, but the pressure of his heavy body was only pinning me down. He went on to beating me with his entire lower arms, while I was silent with shock, blocking myself. I tried using my legs to kick him off me, but he started focusing on my legs too, and started beating them purple. I stretched myself out on the bed and I lifted my upper body up to force him off me with my hands, but he grabbed me and twisted me around to have my face on the edge of the bed. He pinned my entire body down on my side, forcing me in the most uncomfortable position I had ever lied down in. It felt like my bones could break any minute. He wasn't satisfied. He locked my head down over the edge, a quarter of my face on the bed, with the rest of my head in the air, inches away to fall on the wooden frame that was holding the mattress. He rested his arms on my head to put his body weight on it, then he shifted himself to choke me while I gasped for air. Just in case it was my death, I hoped to go straight to Heaven. It got to a point where I was unable to breathe in anymore air, and I was unable to exhale. I felt the block in my throat. I didn't know if I could breathe anymore, so I prepared myself mentally to leave the world. I closed my eyes and he finally stopped. He let go of me and I breathed. I was still alive. Maybe I was asking for too much for our clothes to be perfect on our wedding reception, but I wasn't sure if I deserved that.

For the next two days, I didn't say or do much of anything but stay in the bedroom to heal. I was so stressed and in pain, it felt like I was physically shutting down. Then, the following morning was our wedding reception. I was covered in marks and bruises from head to toe, and I still didn't feel ready at all. In fact, even worse than ever.

I felt physically weak, but I knew I couldn't show it at the reception. My entire face had swellings and marks all over. I had planned to wear very light makeup for the reception, but I knew I couldn't and I shouldn't that day. I caked up my face to cover all the marks as much as possible, and when we went to the venue, my aunt in-laws told me that I looked so pale. One of them gave me her bright lipstick for some color. I didn't even like the color, but I needed to fix something. I couldn't even feel clear-headed at the time. I was on auto-pilot mode, to help cope with the tribulation.

During the reception, for at least six hours, Khatijah wouldn't allow us to sit down or to even eat. I was in heels, and I had to walk around greeting people the entire time with all the pain I had all over my body. The only time I was able to sit down was when I greeted my mom and my brothers. That was the best time I had. I felt safest with them.

The photo collage they had played on repeat used very few

photos of us, with a sudden single photo of Khatijah on her own, with her obvious moustache that she never wanted to get rid of, on the screen. It seemed odd to me. I hadn't gone to many weddings before that, so I wasn't sure if that was supposed to be normal.

The speech Adam gave was about his love for his mother, and thanking her for the marriage and the wedding. No one really cared about the speech, though. Somehow he wasn't speaking very loud and I could tell it didn't get much of anyone's attention. I knew the microphone was working just fine, because we had other people giving speeches and they were very loud and clear. But with Adam's speech, the crowd was louder and he sounded distant. I couldn't really hear him either, but I read the speech before.

We weren't allowed to walk together, either. We had to go around meeting people on our own for the most part. I was acting happy with everyone, making people feel good and welcomed for being at the celebration of my abusive marriage that I was trying to fix, or end. I was feeling sorry for everyone, for clearly wasting their time at the celebration.

At one point, Adam and I went to Khatijah, as we mutually made our round to the entrance. I greeted her happily and she looked at me, but ignored me entirely. I went to the other side of her to greet her again, touching her arms. She still ignored me. I continued greeting people with her, and at the same time, she immediately swung her arms aggressively to the side and behind her where I was, hitting my head hard like a punch. I called her out but she ignored me entirely. Maybe she hated that I was walking with Adam.

I knew I was too tall that day for her to able to hit my head so hard on accident. My headscarf moved to the side almost completely removed. The straight pins on it scratched my head and were out of place, falling off. I was surprised by what she did. I looked at Adam, who just gave me an innocent smile about it, with a guilty laugh, trying to make it look like it was nothing.

I moved to the side on my own to fix it, sitting down, and calling one of my cousin-in-laws to help me afterwards. After I was done fixing it, Khatijah turned around to look at me.

"No! Don't sit down!" she yelled.

"Why?" I asked.

"You have to walk around!" she scolded.

"I'm just relaxing for a bit," I said, ignoring what she had done to me.

"You can't! You must walk around!" she continued to scold and pointed to the dining area.

It was a horrible wedding reception, needless to say. But I thanked her and her family regardless.

13

DAMAGED SENSE

It was September, 2014. On the eve of Eid al-Fitr, we were supposed to break our last fast at Khatijah's sister, Aunty Lang's, place. Adam was busy during the day, so he came back home a little bit later than he should have. I was ready to go, waiting for Adam to be done. When we left the house together with Khatijah, everything seemed fine that we were obviously a little bit late. However, when we got to Aunty Lang's, it turned out to be different.

The moment we stepped into the house and started greeting people, Khatijah started blaming me for us being late.

"She made us late!" Khatijah repeatedly said, pointing to me, while greeting people.

"You're always so slow!" Aunty Lang said to me immediately.

I was so shocked, I immediately looked at Adam. He looked back at me.

"Did you hear what they just said?" I asked him. I knew he heard them. I was never late for any of their events.

There was nothing for him to say. What they did was very clear. He was instantly so angry and embarrassed with them, he immediately wanted to leave. We left the house quickly, before we went even further into the living room.

Khatijah kept calling Adam on the phone, and asked him to pick her up too. When he dropped me off at home, he had to turn back around to pick her up and drop her off home, too. She acted distressed when she got home, with her usual desperate, whining expression. But she didn't apologize to me at all.

It was odd that she always seemed to act like she was a victim, after every problem she herself started. It seemed like she wanted to, or have always wanted that. With someone, with anyone at all. It would have been more decent to just remain mature about things, rather than shamelessly hurting me without me doing anything at all to her. When I first heard that she always had problems with the family, that they would attack her a lot, I genuinely thought that the family were just hating on her. That night, I finally learned that she would go to the extent of shamelessly lying, in order to create problems, and in turn, get the attention she always craved for. (However, I didn't know the extent of her lies until later on, which will be revealed later.)

I would have felt very sad that night, if it wasn't for Khatijah's other sister, Chik. She messaged me to apologize for her two sisters' behaviors. I felt better that there was a little bit of decency.

But the nonsense continued.

Our bedroom's bathroom was an attached bathroom, connected to the guest room. Every time we closed the door that's connected to the guest room, it meant that the bathroom was in use. The guest room's main door, also, was always opened, and in the view of Khatijah's bedroom. It was only a few steps away.

Khatijah had a thing to turn off the water pump every night at midnight. However, a few times, she turned off the water pump when I was in the shower. She also turned off the bathroom light when I was in it. Both, happened at night, and even during the day. Sometimes I had to wash my shampoo off with slow running water, in a long time.

When I confronted her about it, she made excuses for them, mostly in the lines of, "Oops, sorry I didn't know you were in there". But of course I was in there. The door was closed, right? But as my fixed answer, I chose to be patient with her and let it go.

In addition, every time Khatijah came back from her religious classes at night, she slammed the kitchen cabinets, the cupboards, and the doors downstairs. All the slamming happened after the religious classes.

I was doing research in the bedroom in peace and total silence, then I got shocked from the first slam of the front door. The rest of the slamming from the kitchen cupboards and laundry room continued on for a few minutes longer, until what seemed like her rage had finally stopped.

In the first few seconds of it, I thought she was trying to kill something she saw, like maybe a roach. But I've seen her reaction to roaches. She would just casually tell Adam to get rid of it, even if it would take him a while to finally do it. I also knew from the first slam, the slamming of the front door, that it wasn't anything normal. It made me jump a little bit, every time I heard it.

I always knew there was no need for me to rush downstairs to all the slamming. I'm pretty sure it's obvious for even a toddler to know that the sounds are from nothing but anger. There was nothing pleasant about it. So I kept ignoring it every time it happened, hoping she would get over it herself. But in the back of my mind, I thought it was best to accept the possibility that she's purposely doing it to make me feel uncomfortable. As it did, after all, give me a shock every time. It was psychologically disturbing. However, what I didn't think about, was that there's a major possibility she has always been that way even before I moved in. Similar to what I figured with the banging of our bedroom door.

Nonetheless, after a few weeks of the slamming, I couldn't take it anymore. I ran downstairs while she stopped the slamming at the same time and on her way to sit down in the dining room.

"What? What's going on?" I immediately asked her as I got to her, looking at her sternly. I felt like the older one.

"Huh," she looked at me and made a silent sound under her breath. She was shocked and speechless, as she brought her glass of water to her mouth, not looking at me.

"What's going on? Why are you slamming everything?" I asked again sternly, just as loud.

"Nothing," she said quietly, while shaking her head, looking away, and drinking her water slowly in a sip. She was hesitant to talk to me, but she didn't even look upset about anything. It seemed like she just had some fun slamming all the doors for weeks like a maniac.

I went back upstairs to continue my work. It hurt me to have to speak to her that way. There were definitely psychological disorders associated with her crazy destructive behaviors, but that's not what I was looking for anymore. I knew there had to be a reason for her to have developed such condition. There was a beginning to all this. A history.

A few months earlier, sometime at the beginning of the marriage, Khatijah used to say that she couldn't hear my voice. Her hearing aid wouldn't pick up my pitch. It continued on up until suddenly, she couldn't hear me at all. All of a sudden, after confronting her slammings, she was only ever able to hear Adam, her family, and her friends. Most of the time, Adam had to talk to her for me after I would repeat myself louder and louder and I was still unable to be heard. From then on, the only time I was able to be heard was when the conversation would be about something she's proud of, or about something she needed an answer to, or about other people. When we were around other people she knows, she would almost never be talking to me.

I still continued on being myself with her despite all that I was already aware of. I was generally light-hearted with her. I greeted her and smiled at her everyday, and I respected her as my mother-in-law. I persevered in being kind to someone who was persistently being just the opposite towards me. Maybe it was one of the very things she hated. Regardless, she was my mother-in-law, so I was determined to have her quit all the incivilities. And most importantly, to find out why there was so much hate.

14

LOST IN ASIA

It was November, 2014. We were supposed to go to Miri, Sarawak, for Adam's friend, Karim's wedding. I told Adam that if I can submit my thesis on time, then I would be able to go. I needed him to understand that, so that I wouldn't be faced with any more setbacks. After all, I was held back due to abuse once, and the last submission had another bizarre problem, too.

There was technical issue with the printer in uni. It messed up my thesis pages, leaving it with a different format and a random blank page. I found out too late, though, and I still had to submit it. My supervisor allowed me to submit a better copy, but I was unable to make it the next day. I asked Adam if he could submit it for me instead.

"Can you submit my thesis?" I asked him.

"Okay," he answered.

"Print two copies, okay?" I looked at him.

He nodded.

"Here, I'll write it down," I said, while I quickly grabbed a pen and some post-it notes to write down the instructions. I pasted them on a form that was supposed to be attached to my thesis.

"Make sure you print two copies, okay?" I told him again. "You must print two copies."

"Okay," he nodded.

I had his full attention the whole time.

He headed out and I said, "Print two copies!"

When I saw him later on in the evening, I asked him, "Did you print two copies?"

He was wide eyed with his mouths opened, and then he said, "Oops…"

My jaws dropped. I thought he was joking.

"Yeah right," I said.

"No, I forgot…" he said. He was shocked about it too.

I took a deep breath. I exhaled. Men. This must be men.

"How could you forget that? I specifically repeated it so many times!"

"Sorry, I was rushing."

"What were you doing? Next time if you can't then just tell me! I don't *need* your help!"

Once again, I had to write a long apology email to my supervisor, then submitted it myself the following day. Luckily, there wasn't any penalty for it.

I'm not quite sure if Adam's group of friends were just the same, or whether they were slowly becoming like him. I messaged Karim for help once, to get through to Adam. I had the belief that Karim was a beautiful, sensible, and trustworthy Muslim man, as he was the most religious friend of Adam's that I knew of, ever. I was under the impression that we were in the same wavelength, too, as he agreed with me on various topics before.

Adam did his usual running out of the house while ignoring me for no reason, to hurt me, but I knew he was with Karim. He usually met Karim right outside, and they would usually be next to each other sharing stories. All Karim did in response to helping me, was send me religious messages and Islamic verses on respecting the husband. I thought it was rather rude that he was implying I disrespect Adam.

I was shocked by his attitude. As if talking about religion is all that it takes, to help people. Even more so, when a sister in faith is asking for help. A simple help, to reach her husband. I couldn't believe the irony. I've never heard of Islam teaching not to help others. I never bothered to ask him for help since then. When Adam was done with his controlling mode and became nice to me again, he told me not to bother with Karim either. Since then, I became suspicious that his friends would be a lost cause to help me with anything at all, regardless of how much religiosity they would express.

Then on Karim's wedding and honeymoon night in Miri, I learned something new. Adam and I continued to spend time with him, when his newly wedded wife went to sleep. She rarely ever talked with us anyway, even if I directly talked to her.

Karim said, "You know the Islam in Pakistan, that's actually how real Islam is."

Pakistan, where Muslim women have often been shown in the media to be treated like crap? Where the photos of completely disfigured Muslim women are typically from?

"I didn't know Adam's from Pakistan," I answered him right away, sarcastically.

Karim turned to look at Adam with a neutral, delayed reaction, not understanding what I meant. Adam in turn looked at him and just laughed about it. But since then, I wondered why they were fine with acknowledging that real Islam is in Pakistan.

The rest of the time in Miri, Adam and I rented a car and drove around the entire Miri a few times. It was relaxing, but we got bored of it. We decided to visit Brunei for some fun, since it was just next door. We ended up reaching Brunei quite late, though. We drove around and realized that we had to go back before the border gates got locked at 10pm. When we reached the border, it was indeed very locked.

Adam wanted to stay at the border so that we could go through as soon as it would open in the morning. But I had to pee. He asked the guards if we can use the bathroom, but they wouldn't allow that. Which is very understandable. We drove back further into Brunei again. There was a pathway that was out of the way from the main road, and we decided to go in there. There was a mosque that was closed at the time. We drove further up ahead where it was even darker. I peed at the side of the road where there was short but untrimmed grass, facing the woods. It was so creepy, I did it right next to the car.

"Don't tell anyone," I told Adam. "No one knows about this," I said.

I laughed at myself. I remembered a friend of mine peed on the divider grass that surrounded a parking lot, in Malaysia, when everything around us was closed. We just finished work and we were the only two girls with no rides back home. We were in front of a shoplot for goodness sake. I couldn't stop laughing at her. And then we got picked up by someone I was dating. He had no idea he had a girl who just peed in public, in his car.

It wasn't so bad for me, though. I had water and wet wipes to clean myself with.

At first, Adam and I were both worried. We didn't know if it was okay that we were staying past what we told the border patrol. But I figured it didn't make sense for us to get in trouble for it.

"Let's find a budget hotel and stay for a night," I suggested.

"Okay," he agreed.

We searched around for the best hotel to stay at. We searched online on our phones and we inquired some hotels. We didn't like any of the pricing so far. Then we decided to have supper at an open cafe we found. We spent time discussing the differences of Malaysia and Brunei. Things seemed to be okay.

I was actually quite happy with the setback. It was fun that we were stuck there and could do anything we wanted to. It was an adventure. Anything would be good, to me.

We found a hotel with the best price for us. It had colorful lights flickering around the sides of the entrance. A lighted Christmas tree displaying through the glass walls, too. It had a younger feel to it compared to the other hotels.

Adam walked in to talk to the lobbyist. I stayed in the car, watching him. I saw a silhouette of a man behind the counter, attending to him. Then Adam exited, and the man followed behind him to lock the door. Adam switched and seemed moody. He acted up, and didn't even return back to the car. I waited for him and I watched him disappear off to God knows where in the silent night. What was his problem? Did the lobbyist piss him off? Did he not like that we finally found a hotel?

I was not about to walk around on my own like I was forced to in London and Paris. I wasn't sure what Bruneians would be like with me. I presumed they're a lot more conservative. Maybe they would just find it odd to see a young girl all alone at night. I took over the driver's seat. But before I looked for Adam, I needed to be sure everything was okay with the hotel. The way I saw it, anything that pissed him off would piss me off, too.

I knocked on their locked glass door.

"Hi! Excuse me," I said in a rush, waving to a man in the dark.

I waited for a young Chinese man to get to the door. I had a feeling he saw Adam come out of the same car as mine.

"Hi. Yes?" he greeted me. He didn't unlock the door.

We could hear each other through a slight opening about one centimeter between the two closed glass doors.

"Do you have any available rooms for the night?" I asked him.

"Yes, we have one more room available," he answered.

"Okay, thank you. I'll think about it," I said.

He looked at me like I was weird. I was, because I had to be.

There was nothing wrong with the lobbyist, though. I think. And there was nothing wrong with the hotel. I think.

I got back in the car and started driving around. I drove around slowly to look for Adam. I called him at the same time with long pauses in between. I knew there was no point to keep calling if he was obviously receiving the calls but was just choosing to ignore them.

It felt quite nice to drive around there. I still couldn't find Adam. I stopped at more hotels to find more options. I reached a new area further away that Adam didn't get to explore with me. It was spacious and would have been a nice area to relax in together. There were lots of empty roads around. We were married, so we wouldn't even get in trouble if we got caught being out late together. We could've walked around doing anything at all. It could have been fun.

I drove back to where we were, and around the same area a few times, too. I was worried that there were some men hanging out outside a government building in the corner that could possibly have noticed me driving around. I didn't want to look suspicious.

I went back to the same road as the budget hotel we could have checked-in to. I finally found him. He was walking, while I was driving. I flashed the headlights and he looked at me. He ignored me. He went in a random gazebo in front of a shoplot on the same row. He sat on a bench that was in it. It was so dark.

I knew he would sit there for hours doing nothing but randomly wait for me to comfort him. I didn't want to do that though. That's so boring. I parked the car and waited for him. I called him and he still wouldn't answer. I got so annoyed, I decided to drive around on my own again for about 15 minutes. When I got back, he finally wanted to get back in the car.

I had to pee again. I drove to a parking lot where there was a public bathroom. The bathroom was scary, quite similar to some of Malaysia's public bathrooms. I freshened up a bit.

I went back to the car. Adam still couldn't relax. He was stiff and moody. I thought maybe it was because he would have to deal with his mom's usual emotionality, for being stuck in Brunei.

"Don't worry, your mom will understand," I told him.

"What my mom... It's the border, not my mom," he said.

"Okay? Well we can't do anything about it now, can we? So what's the problem?" I answered.

I almost wanted to come to the conclusion that Adam was just really bad at travelling. My dad was a traveler, whether it was for work or leisure. I grew up with a lot of family trips, at least once a year. It really wasn't a big deal that we were stuck in another country, especially that it was the neighbor of our home country, too.

Adam showed that he just wanted to sleep. I hoped he realized that it was silly to sulk about the closed border for so long. It was obvious we were both sleepy by then. I was drowsy and I was yawning a lot. So we fell asleep for a bit in the parking lot. But it was hard for me to sleep. I kept hearing strangers walking around. I was being cautious, making sure we were okay. Adam was sleeping just fine. He always slept just fine.

After a while, Adam woke up and wanted to drive. He was better again, completely fine like we had no problems. We drove around, sightseeing the more colorful parts of the city. We eventually went on our way back to the border around five in the morning. It was already opened by the time we got there, so we were able to enter Miri safely and continued the rest of our holiday there.

15

UNWARRANTED ENMITY

I started researching on how to fix a broken marriage, and the components of successful marriages. Reading all the sad stories ending in happiness made me feel positive again. However, I read nothing about domestic abuse ending in happiness.

I shared some of the links I found on broken marriages, to him, but the only response I got in return was, "You think we're broken?" He was hurt.

I answered, "Yes, of course...?" I was puzzled.

He ignored me for the rest of the day, and I remained quiet, too. It was very exhausting to deal with. He wouldn't even bother trying to fix anything. To him, we were just perfect.

After all the positive marriage articles that he rejected, eventually, I started sharing him religious things. I sent him information based on Islam to remind him why abuse is wrong. Especially to me, his wife, who he should have been gentle with in every situation.

I couldn't stop. I was persistent in reminding him every time he was rude to me or oppressed me in any way. I approached him in a way that I was assuming I had done something wrong to him. As if I had annoyed him in some way.

I did it at home one day when we argued, and I told him off, saying, "In the last sermon, Prophet Muhammad reminded us twice to be kind to women. It was the only thing he repeated. That's how important it is. He would never hurt a woman. He would never abuse any of his wives. Even when they nagged at him night and day, every day. He took it as a man. Did he hurt them for it? For being women?"

He got up to leave without notice. Loudly blaspheming God, and then the Prophet, he left the house.

I cried from how brashly rude he was, and I stayed silent for the rest of the day. Not only did Adam have emotional problems, but he had problems with his faith, too. Which, his faith was the very reason I agreed to marrying him in the first place. I would have been fine marrying someone who was completely honest with me on his lack of faith, if I knew Adam was just lying to me. Adam was definitely not the best option I had as a bachelorette, in terms of everything. I was practically, completely conned into marrying Adam. Kudos to him for fooling me, but it's just too bad he didn't know how to play his own game in the end. He didn't even know how to keep me. Or did he really believe abusing me was supposed to be part of the package? Or did he arrogantly think giving me a ring secured a forever? That I wasn't able to get out under Syariah law, a law that was commonly reported in Malaysia to be biased against women?

Eventually, it happened again another day, and this time I told him off with, "The Prophet always talked about treating women kindly. He would never hurt women and he would enjoy having his wife Aisha out with him even when he had meetings with his companions. All men. He would even listen to all his wives' advices kindly, daily. When they nagged at him about anything, he took it as a man," I repeated it again for him to understand what makes a husband. I continued, "He would comfort them. He was gentle with them. He was patient, not by running out of the house every time, not by giving rude silent treatments, but by gentle and kind silence. There's no beating, there's no abuse... The lightest hit you can give me is like that of a toothbrush, and only after you warn me kindly, three times... I never even got any warnings. At the very least, just hit me with one finger. That's all it takes to make me feel aware and embarrassed enough as a woman," I said. "Hit me with a finger. Try it. Hit me with a finger," I insisted. I wanted to be sure he understood what that light hit meant. He then hit me with one finger and looked at me observantly. I smiled. I was laughing a little bit inside. It was going quite well. "See? That's all you gotta do, baby. You have to treat me well, and only hit me lightly."

"You have to treat me well too," he debated, in a serious manner.

"I do treat you well. I don't have to treat you well like you're a woman though. You don't have woman emotions, do you?" I answered.

"Men have emotions too," he continued.

"Yeah, but not like women," I said. "That's why you have to be even more patient with me. That's why you're a man. You're supposed to handle it. If not, then why do you have a wife?"

"You have to obey your husband," he said in stern a way.

"I do obey you and I have been. But in Islam this is only in the matters of religion, not in everything in the world. I can question and refuse everything else, if I want to, or if I simply don't have the mood for it... It's basic human rights. I listened to everything you've said so far. What is it that I didn't respect? You want me to wear a headscarf? You want me to be quiet? You want me to ignore people?" I said, feeling hurt by the lack of appreciation for all I've sacrificed, even in non-religious matters. I continued saying, "You have responsibilities for me. But when I give the same in return, they're not even my responsibilities, you know? I didn't give you all that I did out of any responsibility. They were my personal sacrifices. My choice to give you. You abused me and I still spent on you, cooked for you all those meals, cleaned up after you, comfort you anytime, follow you wherever you want me to, stay home to wait for you, anything. Even if I lift a single cup for you, it's a sacrifice," I said in defense.

He was so angry, as if he felt it was unfair that I had so much benefits. He got up to leave without notice and said, "Fuck Allah and fuck the Prophet." He left the house.

Again, I was shocked. I felt so conned into the marriage. It was so scary. Even my non-Muslim friends wouldn't say something so rude like that to me. None of them, not my Free Thinkers, Atheists, and even Satanist friends. What more my husband, who once made me believe he's such a good Muslim man? He made me believe he was leading me to a better, beautiful life.

Weeks after that, on the day my final thesis was due, I asked Adam when he would be back by so that I could either use the car or he could help drive me to uni for the submission. He was so upset I didn't tell him about it. I did tell him before, but I was too occupied to remind him again since.

"It's okay," I said. "Never mind, it's not a big deal. I can just get a cab if you're not available."

Then it started to rain heavily. I performed my afternoon prayer before heading out to print and submit to the department. By the time I was done with my prayer, the room got really dark and I continued sitting on the prayer mat comfortably in my prayer hijab, next to the bed. Our prayer mat was like a thick yoga mat material, so it was very comfortable to sit on for a long time. I moved closer to the bed like I was cuddling it, in the cozy heavy rain. I opened my laptop to proofread my thesis one last time.

I didn't realize Adam was already home so quickly, because the sound of the heavy rain had filled up the room and covered the sound of the front door when he entered the house. Usually, I was able to know. He surprised me as he came in, while I was still in the same cuddled position against the bed. I had my head turned around to look at him. He immediately started swinging his entire arms on my back, like I was getting beaten with a baseball bat that was made out of wood and rubber combined. He was bouncing his arms away and back again to hit me, repeatedly. I was speechless.

Ten times and counting, I didn't know when he would stop. I was afraid to get spine injury, so I had my back straightened and tightened, hoping to strengthen it somehow. I still had my chest leaning on the side of the bed. I dated a street fighter when I was in Texas, and he showed me how he strengthened his muscles the street fighter way. I got reminded of it in a split second. I needed to keep things positive. I thought to myself that I will be stronger. But I still couldn't take it, of course. I'm no street fighter. I'm a dancer, gymnast, a swimmer. Fights do interest me, but a man and woman fighting? I don't even have fat or muscles on my back. Even my mom calls me 'dainty' and 'feminine'.

I was still so speechless and I didn't know when Adam would stop. Why was he so screwed up? The room was so dark, it felt like I was just having a nightmare. But it was all too real. It was so painful, I imagined blood flowing out of my mouth eventually. I imagined living physically disabled, if I survived. I imagined staying in the hospital. I imagined the wheelchair. It's unfair that he's so much bigger than me and he has muscles. We're practically way off in weight class. What a coward.

Everything was running through my mind at the same time, and I screamed. I screamed like Adam was just a murderer about to kill me. I never screamed that way before. It felt satisfying. He stopped and I continued screaming as I got up as fast as I could, standing on the bed.

I was panting in fear, and alert. I watched him in the dark in front me. He was a silhouette with pale facial features. The rain had become a thunderstorm and it was roaring. It felt like I was seeing evil right before me, with the silent lightning, flickering light in the room. I had chills up my neck. It felt like a horror movie. I didn't want to be the girl that everyone in the audience whines 'aww' about for not being able to get away from the boogeyman.

"I seek refuge in God from the accursed satan," I said to myself, quietly.

"I seek refuge in God from the accursed satan," he mocked me rudely. "Take this off," he growled under his breath. He came at me while I screamed. All at the same time, he pulled the entire top of my prayer hijab off me and threw it on the floor.

I felt like I was being sexually assaulted by my own husband. I didn't know why I couldn't be dressed the way I wanted to, anytime I wanted to. Especially when it's pretty clear I had just performed a prayer.

I screamed right after. No one could hear me through the heavy rain. The thunderstorm was too loud. But even on the bright and quiet days, no one could hear me anyway. Or maybe they could, but no one bothered enough. We had a Chinese neighbor that would scold someone so loud for the neighborhood to hear for a long time, and no one called the cops on him, either. Not even me. When I hear children crying, I do call the cops, though. I was always worried about the woman that was getting nagged at, hoping she wouldn't get harmed. I wondered who she could be. His wife? His maid? I could hear her answering back crying sometimes. But she never screamed. If she did, I would most definitely have called the cops. I highly doubt the neighbors think like me, though, even if they heard me screaming. I don't think locals trust the cops very much. I always heard bad reputation of them.

"I'm leaving," I cried, running out of the bedroom. I didn't know how I would leave immediately during the storm. I think Adam knew. He just watched me. I ran downstairs and hid myself in the laundry room while I called my mom. When I finally reached her, she was occupied. I sobbed and asked her to pick me up. She unfortunately could only leave when she was done with whatever she was occupied with.

I didn't tell her what exactly happened. I felt bad to stress her out because she advised us before, to stop getting her involved in our marriage problems. Specifically, to Adam, who constantly messaged her to the point of lying to her, in order to get her to be mad at me. I was appalled by the messages he sent, not knowing where his problems came from. When she answered him back in a diplomatic way, he got really annoyed and blocked her.

We had never seen such behavior in our lives ever before. We were never even used to the blocking feature on the phone, before.

He was trying to control my mom, as well. He would on and off block her so casually, anytime he was unsatisfied with the responses that he wanted from her. It seemed as though he was used to getting his way very easily, in his world.

So there I was, in a dilemma of needing my mom's help, yet not wanting to bother her with my problems at all. She went through enough of our problems, with Adam backstabbing me to her. I changed my mind and decided that it's okay in the end, that I can take it on my own. I had faith that I only needed God. I was always independent, anyway.

Once I was done talking to my mom, Adam was trying to get in the laundry room. I sat on the floor hugging my legs, and I was silent with tears. I had a feeling he was going to unlock the door somehow. I could hear him going through small scraps and things on all the tables, like pens, pins, and keys. He eventually unlocked the door and I got myself to the opposite end of the room by then, facing him. I knew I was still going to be at the house, so I continued being silent and gave him my puppy dog eyes. I acted like I have failed to leave him once again, hoping he would calm down.

"Get out, fucking drama," he said, as if he forgot what he just did. It was crazy.

I also had unfortunately missed my thesis deadline because of it, too. I was unable to submit it on time. It was already past the time, in fact. My back was hurting so much still for the next few months. I was just so relieved it was over and I was fine.

On the phone with my mom that day, in the laundry room, she told me to get in touch with a lawyer. I contacted a lawyer and good friend, Nate, someone I knew I could trust. The first time I called him, I got choked up in anxiety trying to explain the situation. I never had to tell anyone about what happened to me. It was even harder that Nate knows me, the real me, not the suddenly-abused-wife me. It was difficult. I never knew how difficult it was to open up about a broken marriage, even when it was to a lawyer I needed help from. When I told him how I was feeling, he referred me to a lady lawyer he trusts, Tina. It easily got me to trust her as well. Tina and I talked about my situation. She supported me emotionally as well. I met her for lunch and kept in touch with her since then. However, both Tina and Nate were civil lawyers, and neither of them were Muslims, so they were unable to help me with the marriage laws according to Syariah law. I still updated them both when necessary, though.

Because talking to Adam wouldn't work, and a lot of times wasn't even accepted or allowed, I started voicing out my views and my concerns of civilization to group chats that we were both in. But they were often left ignored, because he didn't care, and he instead told me to ignore the people I was chatting with. He ignored what he was really supposed to pay attention to. I started talking in various ways, trying to get through to his head, too, but they were always ignored.

The following semester of uni was the beginning of our second year together. I started working on my thesis again for the second time, and for the final submission. This time around I was more distracted than ever to work on it, because of the constant abuse I had to go through and my need to fix it. I knew I couldn't afford to waste any more time as I already have with my studies. I tried my best to focus, but we were fighting so much.

I decided to stay at my mom's for a week, to take a break from Adam. We didn't contact each other for the whole week until I did at the end of the week. It was just a little too odd for me to be silent like that when married. It just didn't make sense. It seemed improper, to me. I was so stressed that week that I brushed my hands lightly through my hair while talking to my mom and I had chills up my spine, seeing what was in my hands. It was a chunk of my hair! I was so stressed that I was losing my hair so easily. I looked at my mom in shock and she looked back at me. I saw in her eyes that she was worried and creeped out at the same time.

I've reminded Adam of what he did to me, and I've even asked him many times to stop abusing me, with his only responses being in the lines of, "I didn't abuse you" and "You're overreacting". I came back home to Adam and he surprised me with another beating that was more tolerable. I tried to get some sense into him.

"Why don't you have any respect?" I asked him.

"Oh, I haven't done anything good for you?" he asked me.

He was irrational, moving the topic even further away from the main problem. That is, him treating me like a punching bag for his life's frustrations, when the Prophet has clearly said to treat women kindly. The very lesson he kept mocking and rejecting every time.

"Did I say that? Do you have woman emotions? You need me to treat you kindly, like you're a woman, for you to understand? What, are you gay? Is that why you don't know how to love a woman? Is that why you try so hard to impress your guy friends every night and you tell me that a woman would only make it uncomfortable there?" I mirrored his anger quickly, but I ended up really wondering if he was gay. One of our college mates asked him if he was gay before, too. Even though he hated gays, and said that they shouldn't be accepted at all. I still wondered and said, "Yeah, that's why Sandra thought you were gay."

"Eww she was so ugly, she thought she was so hot," he said, while continuing on to insult her and challenging me to use that against him.

I didn't agree, but I thought for a bit remembering other guys telling me the same thing, so I accepted his opinion as genuine. "So? She still wondered if you were gay. Maybe in your character. Maybe because all you know is to wash the dishes and clean the house for your mom. That's all you can do. You don't go to work. You don't know how to respect women and to take care of your wife. You can't even get your own mother to respect you and your marriage."

Then I recalled even more of our history when we were just friends in uni.

I said, "Oh yeah, you used to always backstab your ex-girlfriend too, the whole time you were with her. That's why everyone believed she was so crazy and clingy, bothering you so much, when actually you would manipulate everything to make it look that way. For you to have all these fantasies of love, because you never had any. Girls wanting you so much, you're such a great lover that girls would get *crazy*?! And then you said she cheated on you, but you cheated on her first and changed the story? You came to see me, and *then* she cheated on you. You said she went to the clubs without telling you, but you were there too, hanging out with *me*."

"She cheated on me first," still insisting so. I didn't want to focus on that as I didn't even actually care what happened. I just wanted to make a point of how he manipulated women.

"You were so obnoxious in uni, girls just thought you were a *clown*. You were just entertainment. Other guys were so smart, they had so many admirers. But you? You think girls say 'Oh my gosh he's so funny I like him so much!'? Even I never had a crush on you. I really never did," I said, just to add a little more salt to the wound. It wasn't just him. I was usually too focused to have crushes on guys, anyway.

"You think I care about people in uni? You think they know me? What, just because I put up a front with them? They can't even handle serious topics," he said, because we were always light and joking about in uni. Then he continued to ask me, "Who said things about me… Mia? Look what happened to her, her wedding got cancelled. Hilda? Divorced. Lisa? Ew, please, she thought she was so hot and she was so desperate for attention. You think I care about any of the ugly girls there?" he said in disgust, while thinking of more girls we mutually knew. Obviously I wasn't going to confirm with him. I didn't want more guilt.

"Last I heard, Lisa was going to marry *Robert*," I said, making it clear that some people were still having greener grass. Robert was a tall, hairy, big and buff college mate who was just so charmingly attractive. He rode a motorbike too, like Adam, plus he was so decent and such a gentleman. Other than his height and skin color, he was quite the opposite of Adam. I bumped into him once after marriage. It was after a late meeting I had and he told me about his plans for marriage. He was still so pleasant.

"Yeah, and you said so yourself, he wanted to see you that day," Adam said. He reminded me of the connection I had with Robert. Robert's a foreigner, and I had a soft spot for him. I always empathized foreigners a lot. It's not easy. Sometimes people just aren't as welcoming as they should be. Robert and I cared about each other as good friends, and he told me that I was his first good friend in Malaysia. I had to tell Adam about Robert wanting to see me, because Adam was with me at the same time. "You wanna talk about people in uni?" Adam asked. "You don't know what people have said about you."

"Say it then, tell me. See if there's anything new I haven't heard before," I challenged him to surprise me, even though I was already hurt.

"You don't know what they said about your slutty reputation," he said.

I knew I was a 'slut' since the moment I started going to campus. By the second week of enrolling into the university, I was receiving random calls and messages from college mates and complete strangers, too, which was odd, of course. But they all ended up being my friends. I've always been the type to accept people the way they are, so it wasn't a big deal to me. In the same week, however, words quickly spread that I'm a 'daddy's girl', and a 'slut', even though I've been fatherless if I remember correctly, and I had no lover yet. Way different from my reputation at the International school as the 'hot new girl', 'hard-core American', and 'badass bitch'. I didn't even do anything to get that reputation, either. Maybe I had a Texas aura, for both institutions that had two very different perspectives. In the private university, I evidently had to deal with a lot of jealous girls, and dramatic boys who would get defensive, causing problems if I didn't accept their love for me. I knew I had to keep in mind of the different perspective that I was suddenly surrounded in, a perspective Dee warned me about. The *typical Malaysian* perspective.

"Tell me then, tell me more," I suggested. "Tell me how slutty I am."

"Yeah, yeah… everyone hates me, everyone likes you," he said, sarcastically. He gave up.

"I never said that..? Why are you putting words in my mouth?" I scolded, annoyed with how he would jump from one topic to another like he had no care about communication. Not even the biggest sigh could end how irritating that was.

It made me realize that it was so easy for our discussions to jump from one topic to another, with no focus. I didn't realize how we were also so easily distracted from the main problem. Anything about abuse was always ignored, but anything else was fine to be entertained. I didn't realize how much time I was wasting, on trying to make him grow some sense.

It was undeniably not enough for me, because I was still with him. I knew I couldn't live with him and I couldn't deal with our differences. I still didn't have feelings for him. He used to tell me that real love only comes after marriage. I totally get that. I understand that view, but I couldn't see how that would work after all the abuse. If there was a love scale, my love for him never went past zero. All it has been was abuse and mercy, abuse and mercy, and abuse, and mercy.

"What do you think of divorce?" I asked him. It was starting to feel like a standard conversation for me. I knew there was major probability he would go nuts about it, but couldn't he just try and be logical for once?

He was silent.

"We can go back to our peaceful lives. You can find the right one for you, and I can find the right one for me. I would even help you with that, I'll support you. I'll look for a girl for you. Anything at all. We can still keep in touch and continue being good friends," I suggested encouragingly. He was still silent, listening. I thought it was working. He was listening a lot. Maybe he would finally consider. "We can both be happy. And I'll be happy for you."

"Don't say the D word," he warned me.

"I just don't feel any love between us," I said. Why couldn't he just see that abuse doesn't equal to love? "I do want a divorce."

"Divorce, divorce, divorce!"

He punched a cupboard door. And another. I was feeling sorry again. But it felt unfair that I had to be asked for sympathy that way. He was breathing in anger, like he could breathe out fire.

"I still want a divorce…" I insisted.

"Okay, I divorce you," he said.

Then he left the room.

I immediately searched for the Syariah court's number online. I found it and I called. As I waited for someone to answer, I curled by the side of the bed on the wood floor. I was surrounded by my things with no storage space in the corner. I hoped everything will be okay.

"Hello, how can I help you?" It was a lady.

"Hi, this is the Syariah court…?" I asked, nervously.

"Yes, how can I help you?" she answered.

"I'm divorced…" I said. I was shaking. Tears filled up my eyes.

"Okay," she said, sounding a little bit amused in her voice. Maybe it was silly of me to call like that. "Have you ever filed it at the court?"

"No…" I answered. I was secretly crying. I couldn't really talk.

"How many times did you get a divorce?" she asked.

"Twice."

"And you never filed them before?"

"No, I don't know what to do…"

"You're still with him?"

"Yes... He hits me. And he keeps asking for me back immediately after --"

I heard Adam walking to the room.

"Sorry, I'll call back," I said quickly and I hung up. I wiped my tears quickly and acted like I wasn't doing anything. Adam came in the room to ask for me back. A few minutes later, the Syariah court tried to get in touch with me, but Adam was next to me. I couldn't answer. And I never called them back. We went through the typical round of him playing the role of begging for me. I had no time for anything else, and once again, I allowed myself to trust that Adam wouldn't be as terrible as he was that day.

16

MISERY HISTORY

It was 2015. I was done with my thesis and Adam was back in uni to continue his studies. He spent more time out than in by then, for group assignments and meetings. There was more peacetime that lasted longer at home. I spent time working on a new website for my waffle catering, this time without a developer. I was researching on how to do it myself. I needed to, because I didn't want to risk more loss with the developer as I did in the first year. It would be horrible if it had to happen again.

Once in awhile when Adam expressed his stress and anger towards me, I offered him help with his assignments and studying. He always rejected them and continued to work on his own. It wasn't a big deal to me that he was acting that way. It was much more tolerable as there were no physical abuse.

He was having a shower one night when his phone was receiving messages. When I checked it out, as I randomly did sometimes, I saw that a female college mate of mine, Alicia, was messaging him. I immediately got upset, not because she was messaging him, but because I knew since then that Adam was lying to me. He probably hid a lot from me. He told me nothing about girls in uni, the entire semester, and it was already towards the end of the semester. He was to have his final exams soon. He always only talked about the boys.

When Adam got out of the shower, I pretended I didn't know who she was and I kindly asked him why he didn't tell me about her.

"Hey, someone messaged you... Alicia. Why haven't you told me anything about her?"

He didn't want to answer me. I thought it was odd. He completely ignored me while drying himself up with his towel.

Again, I asked him kindly. "Um, why haven't you told me you know a girl in uni..?"

He still completely ignored me and remained silent. He continued to get dressed. It hurt me.

"What…? Why are you not answering me…?" I asked him, confused.

He still gave me absolutely no answer. I felt that he was enjoying doing that to me.

Why was he like that? It was quite pathetic. I had strong feelings that there was nothing happening at all between him and Alicia, and that he just wanted me to think that there was. People who love drama just do puzzling things like that. I never saw Alicia as the type that would be a desperate side whore who would be discreetly cheap with a married man. When I first met her, she seemed like such a sweet, clever girl. But it's possible she could have still had a crush on Adam, though. Or she could just be friendly, as I remembered her to be.

I started boiling in anger with how Adam was behaving. Heat rose up to my face. I felt that he was purposely doing that to me, to test me. He was testing me for all the times I asked for divorce, and for suggesting that he goes with another girl. I took it as a challenge from him. I wanted to play his game and test him back in return. I accepted that he was a mute asshole, and I chose to be patient.

Then, I eventually discovered from his assignments that he was lying about his group members, as well. There *were* girls, but he never once said there were any. He specifically only named the boys. I didn't know why he had to do that. Everything about hiding the girls were so irrational, to me. So what if he had girl friends? Even in Islam, the Prophet had female companions, too. Men and women can still be friends. Heck, even I wished I still had my guy friends to talk to. At the very least, to keep me sane from all that I was going through with this jerk.

Adam got me more and more enraged with this thought, because, not only did he *lie* to me a lot, he would also rather do all this deranged nonsense than to just let me go already! Why did he seem so desperate for an emotional reaction from me? I continued keeping it to myself. I found that he was talking to more girls in uni on his phone. I contacted the girl that messaged him, Alicia, and told her to not be shy to ever talk to me. I would have contacted the other girls too, but I didn't even know them.

Afterwards, I called him the next day when he was in uni. He answered a little bit late. I was on the way there after a meeting I had nearby. He should have been done with his class by that time.

"I'm in the area. Should I stop by to meet you?" I asked him.

"Oh I'm just leaving class now to go to the tutor's office. And I'll be having a group meeting after, so I'll be busy till evening."

"Oh okay, see you later then. Do you want anything to eat when you get back?" I asked.

"No, it's okay, I'll have something later," he said.

I trusted him, I really honestly did. But I still wanted to surprise him anyway since I was really in the area. Plus, I was onto something important, even if I didn't know what I was going to do anyway. I got there in just about three minutes later and parked the car. I had a funny feeling as I got there. I went up to the campus café from the parking lot, and I immediately saw Alicia, the girl that was messaging him the other night. She was a short girl, thin, with long, curly, thick hair. She was so nice as we had always gotten along. She was happy, hyperactive, and chatty. I was glad to see her there. She told me about what Adam was up to.

"Have you seen Adam?" I asked her. We were both sitting on dining benches, directly across each other.

"Yeah! He was just here, eating," she said. She pointed to the messy plate in front of me. He what? I was so shocked, looking at the plate. Adam lied to me again. He was on a roll, wasn't he? I didn't know the cafeteria was his classroom. I wasn't prepared for that. I had no idea what I expected.

"He just had this? He's at the tutor's office, right?" I asked her calmly, to confirm.

"Uh yeah..." she looked at the plate, probably wondering why I wanted to confirm that. "He just left like five minutes ago," she told me. I didn't know how to control myself anymore. I felt so disrespected.

I was shaking when I messaged Adam so fast and said, "Where are you? I'm with Alicia now and she told me everything."

I continued talking to Alicia about other things, but I was distracted. I kept checking my phone for Adam's response. Every time I checked our message box, I felt anger. Disrespected.

Adam finally got back to the cafe. He was with Jose, a male mutual friend of ours. He was surprised to see me. He didn't check his phone yet. I moved in, to sit further in the bench, for him to sit down. Jose sat in front of me.

"So, what are yall up to now? Group meeting?" I asked them.

Jose and Alicia both thought about it and shook their heads, saying, "No..."

"I live so far away and I don't even have my laptop with me," Alicia said.

"Yeah, I'm not prepared with anything either," Jose said.

Then what the heck was Adam talking about? What meeting?

I looked at Adam calmly, to my right, to see what he had to say about it. He acted calm, watching Jose and Alicia, too. I kept looking at him as we continued sitting there, talking about nothing. Adam didn't want to talk at all.

Then he randomly asked for the car keys and quickly said, "Let's go."

He got up to leave straight away. We all said bye to each other, and left.

I think I know what Adam wanted out of that. My theory is that it was a fantasy.

First of all, he wanted to prove to me that girls in uni were indeed attracted to him. That they would try to be his friend, even when he's married. Just as how Alicia was talking to him a lot, even directly, but he showed that he didn't really bother to answer her much, or that he just didn't care.

Second, not only did he not have a meeting, but all he wanted was just to hang out and do nothing. He wanted to hang out at the café, as he usually did for years when I used to see him and meet him at the café. It was an activity for him. It's very typical of Malaysians to do that as an activity, daily. They call it 'lepak', an activity of sitting somewhere together and almost literally do nothing for hours. Throughout the years of going to uni, Adam was always seen 'lepaking' at the café. Pretty obvious that's what he wanted to do, but he instead told me he had a meeting. Why lie about it? And how often has he lied to me just to 'lepak'?

Thirdly, which was what pissed me off the most, was that I was forced in that same position he put his ex-girlfriend in. I remember when his ex-girlfriend came to visit him in campus. Everyone judged her so harshly. She was crazy, she hated every girl Adam knew, she was this and that. I walked past Adam walking with her once, and he stayed slightly behind her to give me a gesture to not talk to him. I thought it was so odd, considering Adam would have to go to uni and meet many people anyway. It was then my turn to be the main girl in his life, supposedly caring so much about him to the point of going nuts. When in fact, he had manipulated me to search for a simple answer that he shamelessly refused to give. A simple answer, to a simple question of why he didn't mention any girls. And why he couldn't just let me free, too. How pathetic.

I was aware of what was happening, and I couldn't stop myself from feeling horrible. The feeling of disrespect that I felt can't possibly be described.

On the way back home, I asked him for a divorce. I knew we didn't have to talk about whatever happened. We were both well aware of it enough already.

"Why don't we just divorce…?" I asked him, confused with our situation.

He seemed so angry, but he didn't answer. He just had a serious face on. We were driving quite slow through the traffic. He turned into the first neighborhood we could turn into, and found some neighborhood shops to park the car at. I thought he wanted to talk properly. But he got out of the car to leave me there. He started walking into the neighborhood. I turned off the car and I quickly followed him. He was walking so fast.

"Why are you being so childish?! How old are you?!" I asked him from a few meters' distance behind him. "Why are you ignoring me?! Why is it so hard to discuss divorce?!" I asked him, already reaching him. He turned around quickly to change the direction and continued on walking faster. "Why do you wanna go through stupid shit like this?! Do you have any logic at all?!"

He was silent the entire time. I left him. I walked back to the car and started the engine. I found him walking across the road from me, suddenly. He wasn't in the neighborhood anymore. He was walking on the sidewalk across the road from me. I caught up to him and parked the car further up ahead where he was walking towards. I opened the passenger door for him to get in, but he ignored it and past me. I shut the door. I honked quickly. I drove by him slowly with the windows rolled down.

"Hey! Get in!" I yelled out to him. He ignored me. He crossed the roads, back into the neighborhood again. I turned the car around and followed him. I wasn't going to be the bitch wife that leaves my husband stranded, that's for sure. I know he abandoned me a lot of times, but I could never understand that.

He led me all the way to the end of the road, where I would end up back into the highway, and on the way back home. I knew I was stuck there, that once I continued into the road, I wouldn't see him again until a very long time. He would have to find his own way back home. I looked at the back of his head and I thought I had to leave him there, as much as I would sympathize it.

Then all of a sudden he switched. He was fine to get back in the car. The chaos ended like nothing happened. I drove us back home silently through the traffic.

When we got home, we were both exhausted. I sat on a sofa in the living room. Adam was putting down his bag in the dining room. I took it as an opportunity to have a calm discussion, finally.

I asked him, "Why did you have to lie to me? Why would you rather sin and lie to me, than get a peaceful, permissible divorce?"

He started blurting out what seemed like random words, loudly. Gibberish coming out of his mouth so loud, like he was chanting. He walked around back and forth in the living room in front of me, near the front door. Maybe he was thinking of running off again. But I knew he was exhausted from what we just went through. And I knew he wanted to block me out. He didn't want to hear me talk about divorce. It was too annoying for me, though. Creepy, too. I acted like I wasn't creeped out, just in case.

"Oh my gosh… do you see yourself…?" I asked him, while still relaxing on the sofa.

"I don't give a shit," he answered me. He continued on with what he was doing.

"I'm recording this to send to my lawyer. You're ruining it more for yourself," I said. I just wanted him to calm down and have a mature discussion with me for once.

"Send it then," he said. I recorded him as he continued on with ranting. I didn't actually want to send it to any lawyer. It was so stupid. I just really wanted him to stop.

He looked at me and realized that I really was recording him. He didn't like that. He came over to me and grabbed my phone out of my hands. He grabbed onto my right hand and dug his thumb into my palms and twisted it. My left hand tried to remove his hand off me, but I couldn't. He blocked me. I used my legs to push him off and he was blocking my legs while he tried twisting my right arm. I pushed his face with my left hand and he grabbed both my arms tightly. I applied my body weight onto him to push him off. He grabbed me and pushed me down to the floor on my knees. I crawled away from the sofa and got myself up quickly. He came towards me at the same time as I walked backwards to a wall behind me, watching his moves. He choked me while carrying me up against the wall. I was choking. My neck felt swollen and I couldn't breathe.

I prepared myself mentally to die there. My last dying thoughts. Dear God, please bring me straight to Heaven. I couldn't believe that was the end of my life. Murdered, in the hands of my husband. Would anyone ever know he killed me? Would he get away with it, like everything else he did to me? Would it be out in the news? What would the story be? I saw a newspaper in my mind. I was ready to leave. I didn't have time to think anymore. It was over for good.

Then he let me go. I breathed.

He immediately went to the sofa to rest, then closed his eyes. I was exhausted, too, so I went straight to the sofa next to him. I could have passed out there. We were both silent.

I gathered enough energy in about five minutes. I took my phone that was on the floor, to bring to the dining area with me. I stood by the wall where there was a side table. I searched for the Syariah court's address to go there again, and to ask them to give me the divorce. I hated that I had to do that, because I knew it wouldn't be easy. What would I say to them? Would they take it seriously? The Syariah law system was really annoying me.

"If you don't give me the divorce, I'm getting it myself," I said to him, from where I was standing.

He woke up from his rest and turned around to face me.

"Stop talking like that," he said.

Why couldn't I talk like that?

"I almost died," I reminded him. "Do you not understand what marriage is supposed to be like?" I asked him.

"What do you want? I'll give you anything you want!" he yelled out to me.

"What do I want?" I asked him in disbelief. "I want a husband that won't abuse me. I want a mature husband. I want a husband that knows how to talk to me when we have problems," I told him.

"What problems? What do you wanna talk about?" he asked, highly confused.

"How about the problems of you lying to me?" I suggested.

"What lies? I didn't lie to you!!!" he cried out in frustration.

"You lied to me the *entire* semester. Why? Why did you feel the need to lie to me? You want all those girls? You like them? Do you wanna be with them? Is that why?" I asked him, seriously. "'Cause it's okay if you want them, you know. I just don't know why you wanna hold on to me," I made it clear to him.

"I didn't lie to you!!!" he still insisted.

"See? You can't even talk," I pointed it out. "You can never talk properly, and you would deny everything anyway. What's the point? How can we ever improve? We never can. It's always about your stupid problems and treating me like shit. You don't have to tell me about any girl. I just want a divorce."

"I don't want a divorce!!!" he cried and dropped his knees to the floor.

"You still can't fuckin' talk properly!!! Are you purposely doing this? What is it that you're trying to protect? You're trying to protect the girls? Are they your responsibilities?"

He got confused, asking in loud breaths, "Huh? What?"

"You lied for an entire semester and I had to find out everything myself! Even Alicia told me the truth!" I reminded him in frustration.

"I didn't lie," he answered in confusion, again.

I had it with him. I let out a big sigh.

"Just go ahead with that broomstick," I said. I insulted Alicia, to release more frustrations on him. It was horrible of me, but I had to make the point of him lying to his own wife for any Tom, Dick, and Harry.

"I don't want that ugly midget with annoying voice!!!" he yelled out in anger with tight fists.

I told him clearly, "Well that's not my fucking problem. You've been abusing me, and now you've been lying to me. I'm getting my divorce."

"No!!!" he yelled out for a few seconds. "I'll do anything for you! I'll give you anything you want! Please!!!"

"I want a *real* marriage!!! Do you know what a marriage is?!" I answered back, frustrated with him so much I had my teeth locked and my fists clenched, too. "Marriage is not just about yourself! It's about two people! There's someone else in your life now! Can you be truthful? Can you be gentle?!"

"Yes! I won't lie to you! I'll be gentle. I promise I'll be better! Just give me a chance! I don't want divorce," he said. Then he started crying and sobbing, looking down, while saying, "I do everything for you... Anything you ask, I give it to you... I'll give you anything... Anything..."

I watched him there, as usual, wondering how he can cry for me so easily. He could have cried a river. I let out a big, long sigh. I went over to him and I rubbed his back. I ushered his heavy body to stand up, to sit on the sofa again. We sat on the sofa. I watched him crying with his head down. I just watched him curiously. Then I continued to rub his back and pet his head. I hugged him. I allowed his head to rest on my neck and chest while I cuddled him. We could have fallen asleep there. A few minutes passed. Through the bare sliding doors, we saw the house gate opened. Khatijah was home. We got up and went up to the bedroom, ending our day.

In another semester, we met a group of the other girls he was hiding from me. It was easy for me to tell who was new in his life, in uni, because I knew him for years there. I practically knew everyone that he knew there. He agreed to participate in an interview for my Psychology of Religion project. When we were about to leave the campus, we were greeted by the girls.

They were standing at about two meters' distance from us. The shortest girl, who seemed happy and bright, talked the most.

They briefly told each other what they were up to in uni, then she eventually asked if I was his wife.

As we walked to the car, I asked him casually, "Why didn't you just introduce them to me?

"Huh?" he asked, immediately defensive. I knew he would already start to annoy me, but I had to continue.

"We had to introduce ourselves...? She had to ask about me?" I reminded him. It was supposed to be a simple conversation. Couldn't he just be charming or funny about it? It's not like I was emotional. I was only asking.

Then he suddenly said, "I knew you would be like this."

He ran off without warning to a shoplot. I was unfamiliar with the area, because it was a new relocated area for the uni at the time. So I chose not to look for him. I called him, though, but he clearly and persistently refused to go home with me. I didn't want to bother with him like I did the last time we were from uni. I didn't want anything similar to that at all, so I left him there as he wished, and I went home on my own.

17

DOUBLE BABBLE

During Adam's semester in uni when he was lying to me, concurrently, every time he wasn't home, I randomly heard the same pitch of a single sound. It surprised me every time. Sometimes it happened a few times in a row. Every day that it happened, I wondered where it was from. It sounded like a message notification. It bothered me for many days. I waited for something to happen on his computer, but there was nothing. I turned up the speakers, and I even stood by the windows to see if it was from any of the neighbors. It was getting really annoying because it only came up randomly while I was busy working. Always when I was concentrating. I eventually asked Adam, but he didn't know what I was talking about. I tried explaining to him, but he didn't really bother with it.

Until suddenly, I found that Adam would leave a messenger app running on his computer, that was using Cloud operating system. I was sure that *that's* where the sound was coming from. The app was completely open on the desktop for me to see, this time. Did Adam finally decide to just leave it open for me, wanting to show me something? He was actually receiving messages all this while, and some of the chats had notification sounds enabled. I felt like Pandora's box was calling me all this while. It was now welcoming me. I didn't even do anything yet, and I felt mischievous.

I went through the app like it was research material. I always vainly thought I'd be a great detective. One quote I always lived by since I was a kid was, "The truth will always prevail". I told Adam that before, too. It keeps me calm through hateful people who try to sabotage me.

I discovered Adam was right about some of his friends being filthy perverts. It wasn't very fun going through those messages. It was just like seeing some boys going through puberty and never got over it. They're all around thirty years old, for goodness sake. Anyway, I didn't bother with his friends much.

Nevertheless, my most significant finding was from the messages Adam had with his mom. I found out that all this while, Khatijah has been creating *lies* about me. She was even implying things that I apparently have done. Apparently, I've been quite the monkey jumping around in the house, messing up her entire house and forgetting to throw my own trash in the bin and not washing my own dishes. She sent many photos of crumpled tissues and other sorts of trash to Adam, too. I never saw that much trash before, but when I did, I just threw them away. I always wondered why Khatijah couldn't just throw them in the bin when the trash would be directly in front of the bin. Just as she left all her dirty dishes in and around the sink every day, I assumed she just didn't have the time.

The fact of the matter is that I was washing the dishes for her everyday. Every single day she left for her classes, and anytime throughout the day. I had a routine to have breakfast and then wash up everything I saw in the sink, including all the kitchen equipment she would leave in there. There was almost always a blender, because she always made drinks for herself with it in the morning. I even cleared up the kitchen counter, and organized anything I saw. Every day. It was a daily routine for me. It was out of love that I took the time to ease her life, too, not just Adam's. Even Adam wasn't aware of this, because I never felt the need to point it out. It was sincere. But, how magical was it for them, to have a clean kitchen when they came home every day? What a miracle! It was clear to me then that Khatijah hated anything good about me. Anything good, at all, even if the good benefited her. Maybe it scared her, like the light of goodness scares the devil. Apart from all that she said and did to me for over a year, the messages were enough evidence of it.

Just about every single time Adam was not interested in a family event, or anything at all that had to do with family, Khatijah messaged him about how everyone in the family helped us with our wedding. Every time. Even if Adam was busy with work. She did this as a standard procedure to get him to go every time. And mind you, we met Khatijah's family a few times in a month. At *least* once a month. The wedding in the end was never a gift like she made us believe it to be. Instead, it was a price of slavery for Adam. Adam was forever stuck in the guilt of having the help of family that she constantly used against him. What sort of sick family help was that, then? She talked about him having to pay them back by going for the events. Every time we went for the events, it was almost as if we were the only ones who were always there. Every other cousin we knew were able to live independently, focusing on their lives and the success of their work once in awhile. They never had to attend every event, because no one even really cared about their absence. Adam, however, always had to attend every single event. If he didn't, Khatijah would sulk about it and act like Adam was giving her a hard time. There was almost always highly emotional drama if we couldn't make it to any event. Even as newlyweds. We were the only couple, regardless of age, who never had a breather from their clinginess.

I even found that during our first year of marriage together, after I already told Khatijah that her son had hit me, she messaged him, saying, "If she hits you again then just walk away." Wow! What a joke of the circus! I hit *him*? Adam didn't really say anything about it but he entertained her anyway. Of course he did. Anything to save his reputation. Why not, right? They were most likely so scared that I would open my mouth about it to anyone they knew, especially because I had already asked for divorce at the time. They had to have some defense, which, her only defense was to twist it around to say it was me. This was only a few of the things, among many, many things Khatijah had appallingly twisted.

I even saw a pattern of when she sent these messages to Adam.

They were always when she was supposed to be with a lot of people, such as her religious classes and other gatherings. Funny how she couldn't just tell Adam in person, especially when she saw him and talked to him every day at home, right? It clearly wouldn't work well for her, though. She had to wait for people to be around her, to see her sending *lies* to her son, about me.

Apart from backstabbing me, she even backstabbed *my mom* at random times. She accused my mom of not wanting to be responsible for me. My mom, someone who paid for our entire wedding and hired professionals, and even gave us all the money the guests gave. The only person in our lives who ever bought us a honeymoon, and gave us the choice of where we wanted to go. My mom, a widow of five children, made me and Adam an entire dinner table full of home cooked food, both Western and Asian food, just about every single time we visited her.

Khatijah, a widow of one child, was controlling on our wedding day and even hit my head. Didn't want any input on the wedding planning at all, but couldn't even get one professional photographer that I could have easily hired myself. Kept all the money the guests gave as newlywed gifts, to herself, as a rebate for the wedding. Guilt trip Adam consistently about how everyone in the family helped us for our wedding, throughout the entire marriage. Got us to meet Adam's dad's side of the family, only to share hotel rooms with us as newlyweds, and to give me mean looks around my in-laws. Forced us to eat anything she bought for us with no choice, and any groceries she wanted us to finish at home, daily, that we never even would have asked to have. And she wanted to talk about responsibilities?

My mom has only trusted Khatijah so much as another mother in my life. She never once said a single bad thing about her. My mom never backstabbed and gossiped just as Khatijah liked to do. And this is what Khatijah did to my mom in return. Goodness gracious. It took me awhile to gather all the evidence. I took note of them since then. I saved the things she would say sometimes. I chose to be patient for a while. I waited for a few months, until my patience with her was wearing anorexically thin. She went too far, farther than far.

It was our second holy month of Ramadan together. As usual during Ramadan, Adam and I prayed together with Khatijah in the living room. Adam was the 'imam', the one leading the prayer. Women can't be the imam for men, so Khatijah always prayed beside me, behind Adam.

Like the previous Ramadan and any other day, Khatijah still expressed her anger through low patience. There was not much of a difference whether it was Ramadan or not. She was rarely ever at peace with herself. I sensed her aggressiveness even during prayers. She pushed my arms using her stiff elbows a lot. Just as always, when I prayed next to her.

This time, she was so outrageously rude. She waited for me to be done with my personal prayer to God. I didn't know she was waiting for me. We were both sitting quietly on our prayer mats. Adam was relaxing on the sofa behind us. I thought Khatijah was also focused on praying to God. Immediately when I got done, she turned to look at me and started laughing at me with her hands pointing at me, while accusing me of bowing to God incorrectly.

"Ha… ha… you bow wrongly," she laughed childishly with her hands pointing at me, and continued to laugh like how I bowed was hilarious.

I looked at her as I stood up to roll my prayer mat. I gave her a quick confused expression and carried on calmly with my prayer mat.

She followed me to stand up too, but not focused on her prayer mat. She immediately got her phone that was on a side table, next to the sofa Adam was relaxing on.

"You bow wrongly… ha… ha…" she still laughed while pointing at me.

"What…?" I said to myself out loud. I was so confused by her graceless behavior.

"You always bow wrongly," she said, while acting like she was laughing.

I got more confused, because, how was that so? How would she know that I was bowing incorrectly, if she was praying next to me? Does she have eyes on her sides? Was she not focused on praying to God? Why was she so focused on obsessing over me during her prayers? Strange, was I her Goddess? I seemed to have taken over her obsessions completely, even during her prayers.

She held out her phone to face me while laughing and said, "Do it, I wanna record it."

"What..?" I expressed my confusions out loud again. I felt so awkward and uncomfortable. I looked at Adam to see what he thought of that. Adam seemed to not want to get involved at all. He was just on his phone. I looked back at Khatijah.

"Bow, I wanna record it," she said, while laughing. "And then I'll show you."

I knew she was purposely doing that to me, considering I had already expressed how I was confused by her behavior, and how uncomfortable I was feeling. I would say, only someone seriously stupid would confuse my reaction to thinking I was pleased with the moment.

I looked at Khatijah with seriousness and said, "No, that's okay."

I sat down next to Adam. I ridiculously expected for him to at least say something about it to defend me, and of course he did nothing. I was very disappointed with him. He was a terrible so-called leader for me. He couldn't even handle a simple situation like that. How can a son not be comfortable enough to talk and be honest with his own mother? Khatijah was watching me for a while and then she left us with her chin up in anger. I had a feeling she didn't get the reaction she was hoping for from me, for her daily gossip hour.

Later on, ironically, she told Adam that I can't even act like a family. I never knew family meant 'be rude to each other for no apparent reason even if it violates them'. I always only learned decency and love with family. Anything opposite would be considered a conflict, which would have to be resolved sooner or later, and whether we like it or not.

Gradually, after Ramadan and Eid al-Fitr celebrations, I started telling her off for a lot of things. I didn't bother with Adam anymore, because he seemed too useless by then to defend me against anything. I started figuring things out myself. I didn't care that Khatijah would enjoy the stories of me telling her off, with others. I sent her text messages to be sure that she was receiving my words, regardless. I was quite enjoying telling her off and being sarcastic to her, while she acted like she was a patient person in return with me in the messages, while backstabbing me and manipulating my reputation endlessly. It was great, how unaware she was of my awareness. I wondered why she was such an awful person, thinking she was so clever with her dissembling method.

One by one for months onwards, I told her off for banging on our bedroom door every day and throughout the day, and I told her how sickening it is to live with her aggression and bad attitude, and I told her off for relocating my things without informing me, I told her off for the bowing that she wanted to record, I told her off for walking in the bedroom without any notice, I told her off for controlling Adam to the point of him not having any studies or work time, and I asked her to stop being so rude and pretty much to stop being a jealous cunt, in general.

I can't forget how she ended up copying and pasting something I sent to her, back to me. I immediately knew she wanted to share the conversation with others, so I told her off for that, too. Specifically, for her witless two-faced attitude of backstabbing and gossiping.

"I don't want to spread to others, only to Adam, he's your husband," she said to me.

"There's a limit to how much you can speak of me to Adam, as I am his wife. Speaking negatively or spreading negativity in regards to a man's wife, is destroying his dignity. So please be careful with your thoughts and choose your words wisely even when it's to him, if you have any genuine love for your child at all," I answered her.

I was glad to be able to say that, because in a way, I was able to tell her off for all the times she lied about me to Adam. Something she never knew I knew, from reading her chat, and other observations. I was glad she accidentally did the copy and pasting to me. In the end, I was able to finally say that to her.

She said, "I wanted Adam to explain to me why he told you that he was working for me and not completing his studies."

I asked her, "When did I say he said that to me? There's something wrong with your perspective or with your heart, if you keep enjoying all the negativity, as you have all this while."

"Then why did you say 'working for you and not even complete his studies'...?" she asked me, acting dumb, or just not even acting.

"When did I say Adam said that?" I asked.

"Why did you say that he was working for me, as though that is why he couldn't complete his studies. I gave him all the opportunities to complete his studies before he met you."

That was hilarious. Of course she stopped giving him the opportunity to complete his studies after marrying me! She was so bitter about him wanting to get married, that she never even wanted to support him after! But I didn't answer her.

Even if what she meant was that Adam was doing so well before meeting me, that too was hilarious. Adam was not doing well before he got married to me. I was actually surprised by how well he was doing in his classes, *after* he got married to me. He was much more focused after having me ease his daily life and chores. What a joke that I made it worse for him. I didn't do anything to his studies other than offer him help for anything he wanted at all. Before, and after marriage. Tutoring, studying, tips, notes, books, and anything around the house. Even with all the things I had to juggle for myself.

I told her, "That's a topic you should have continued with me, and not spread lies about me to my husband. Don't be ridiculous and say you haven't been."

She couldn't respond to that.

Then one day, I was able to obtain more data. I was cleaning the bathroom. Adam came home and gave me a very bad feeling from his energy. I felt like I was about to get another random beating. I washed my hands then I looked at him in a serious, defensive way when he stood by the bathroom door. I didn't even know what it was about, if there was anything at all. I can't remember if he used something, or it was just his bare hands, to hit the shower sliding door. He broke the glass and made a hole through it. Maybe he was just enjoying the testosterones he couldn't handle. I do remember cleaning everything up later on, though, and masking up the hole with duct tape.

I imagined getting attacked in the bathroom and hitting my head on the sink or the toilet bowl, or falling and breaking something. I quickly decided to go back in the bedroom, passing him. I continued to give him my serious, defensive expression. He continued to look at me.

"Don't give me that look," he said.

It seemed like that was his problem with me. He hated what I was doing. But I couldn't help it. I knew he would abuse me. Even if I smiled at him, or if I had just prayed, it was still going to happen anyway.

Adam had no idea how much I already knew about him and his mother at that point. All my research done had led me to so much contempt over them. By that time, I held so much resentment for ever loving them unconditionally, only to receive nothing but sadistic treatment in return. I clenched my fist while looking at him in anger.

"I said don't look at me that way," he said.

"Why can't I?" I asked. I locked my mouth and my jaws in anger as my heart beat faster. I was very defensive. I didn't even know how it happened. I hated his face, his energy, and his presence. I felt no sympathy for him or his mother anymore.

"You're still looking at me that way," he said.

"So?" I asked him.

He locked his jaws and pushed me to fall on the bed. He immediately started hitting me, while I covered myself with my arms. I kicked and hit him, and I screamed a lot but he didn't care. He seemed to be more excited to continue, pulling me back to beat me every time I got away.

I was so fed up with everything. When I managed to get myself up and away from Adam and the bed, I left the room and headed straight to Khatijah. I looked back at Adam through the open door to see if he was chasing after me. He wasn't. He stood in front of his bed, unmoved, and watching me, clueless as to what I was doing.

At the perfect timing, Khatijah opened her bedroom door when I got out of the room, too. She stood by her door to watch me, too.

"Hi," I said to her, as I walked fast towards her.

Then when I got right in front of her, I hit her head with my fisted palm. Everything went smooth, like it was meant to be. But I realized I did it so light, she didn't move at all. Even her head didn't tilt. Her head was quite stiff, unmoved. My only regret from it was that it wasn't as hard as she had hit me on my wedding reception day.

To make it any more odd of a scene, Khatijah's face immediately lit up from it, the same way it lit up the first time I told her Adam hit me in the first month of our marriage. I shifted to stand next to her, to see what Adam was doing at the corner of my eyes. Just in case he was coming to attack me for that.

"That's for hitting me on my wedding day," I said, to be clear with her.

Adam was walking towards us slowly. He was speechless, and he too only seemed fascinated with the situation. He didn't do anything when he got to us, and not even the slightest disapproval to me. It was almost as if he believed Khatijah deserved it for disrespecting us and our marriage, and for annoying him a lot, too. I almost felt like I was doing him a favor, as horrible as it sounds. I always wanted to help him somehow, anyway.

Then Khatijah gave her usual desperate, whining expression to Adam.

She asked him, "When, when...?"

Adam looked surprised that she was acting dumb to that extent. He was silent in return. He had no words for her.

I answered for him and said, "On my wedding day, you saw me, and then you swung your arms hard to punch me."

Khatijah only continued her whining with the same expression on her face.

She asked, "When...? I don't remember!"

I knew she was just going to continue on denying, as she normally did with everything else that's dodgy anyway. Adam most likely knew that too. I felt that she was hoping Adam would get angry at me from her whining that way. But he pretty much didn't care.

"Forget it," I told her. I left to go back to the bedroom.

Adam seemed to be so proud of what I had done, that he took me out on a nice dinner date that same night. That was definitely rare. He expressed his love for me more than ever, and shared dreams of our future together. It was so unreal. I didn't know it was so easy for me to be rewarded and get the sweetness that I always wanted from him. All I had to do was be the one to stop his bitch mom. I was spending so much time wondering why he could never seem to stop his mom from being psycho, when all he was ever asking from me was to be the one to do it!

I recalled a time when I got in a girl fight with Sandra, the girl that wondered if Adam was gay. Many people, both boys and girls, saluted me for it, because they all apparently couldn't stand the girl anyway. Adam specifically, gave me the most admiration. He had the most mesmerizing stare on me for the longest time. I thought it was just because he couldn't stand her too, like the others. Well most likely that, too. But that night after hitting Khatijah and being rewarded for it, I wondered if Adam was actually subconsciously wanting me to help him with his nasty situation at home, too. I did want to help him so much, but not by being the one to stop Khatijah for him. I wasn't going to be that person. I've been told I'm selfless, but honestly, not that much. I wanted to help Adam stand up for himself instead.

I felt even more sorry for Adam. My sense of protection over him grew. I really wanted nothing more than to protect him as much as I could. However, I still felt guilty for what I had done to his mother. The more I loved him, the more I naturally had love for his mother, too. Although, I still believe that it was my right to justice. Regardless, it was for spiritual reasons that I wanted to apologize to Khatijah.

When we got back home, walking up the stairs, I told Adam, "I wanna apologize to your mom."

She was watching TV. We honored her and greeted her.

Then I cried, and said, "I'm sorry I hit you, mummy..."

She opened her arms out for me to hug her. I hugged her and rubbed her back.

"Sorry..." I said. I pet her head and kissed it.

Adam and I went in our bedroom and I continued crying while sitting on the edge of the bed. It wasn't easy to apologize to her, especially when I knew how she has been with me, and us.

I wasn't sure how Adam was feeling about the whole thing. He seemed neutral, unaffected.

Things pretty much remained the same after that. Nothing improved. There was no harmony in the home or anything. Khatijah was persistent in making us believe she never hit me. A week later, she held a religious class at the house.

After the class was over, when everyone was socializing, she randomly came up to me.

Khatijah said with a laugh held back, "Next time just tap on my shoulder so I know you're there!" She tapped on my shoulder to show me how to get her attention.

Her saying that to me was just as random as it sounds. I immediately knew she was talking about the time at my wedding when she supposedly didn't know I was next to her and she hit my head.

And yes, actually, I did tap her arms when I attempted to greet her the second time. Shoulder or arms, that was exactly what I did. But by then, I was so tired of her persistence of the same topic she probably planned to deny ages ago, that I just let that old woman have her gossip fun. I knew there was no point anymore and it would only waste my energy. I had bigger problems to solve, than to win a small case shared amongst her dependent support system.

Soon after, one day, we went to Khatijah's friend's son's wedding celebration. It's very easy to remember her friend. She had exactly the same full name as Khatijah, with the same spelling, and even the same last name. She had a very spacious house further away from us, and she shared some things about the architecture. We were treated so well there, with special attention when we dined privately in her spacious back patio.

When we were saying our goodbyes, Khatijah's friend shared stories about Khatijah, of when they were younger. In college. One of them was that everyone used to call her 'makcik'. That was pretty much her nickname. The literal meaning of 'makcik' is auntie, although in the Malaysian culture, it's really just an insult when you use it on a young woman. It's usually just a term for old, traditional Malay women. Using it once or twice by one friend could be considered a joke, but if everyone regularly called her that, then that's a different story there.

It was awkward how Adam, Khatijah, and I, stood there listening to her. Khatijah wanted to walk away, but still stayed, because none of us moved. Adam seemed nervous for his mom. I felt awkward. We were all awkward, except for Khatijah's friend, who was busy and happily telling me stories while I listened.

It was hard to forget what Khatijah's friend shared, especially because Khatijah suddenly started calling the weekly maid that came over, as 'makcik'.

"Makcik is coming today," she said.

"Makcik is coming tomorrow," she said another day.

"Makcik's supposed to be here by now," she continued every time.

She kept using the word 'makcik' so casually to call the maid that, instead of the maid's actual name that we usually called her by. She never did that before. She seemed to be wanting to show me that the term was always used anytime. But I knew it wasn't that way. Her doing that only emphasized my attention to it.

I sympathized her for it, imagining how hard it must've been for her. I've had my awkward stage in life, too. It was during puberty. However, I still had good relationships with others. Boys were so good at sweet talking, and friends thought I was pretty. I didn't even know it was an awkward stage at all because of that. I was so oblivious to the changes I was experiencing. I only realized how awkward puberty was after looking back.

I can't imagine what it would have been like if I had gone through such awkwardness in my college years, to the point of being labelled as a 'makcik' by everyone. It's no wonder that she was always so angry with me. She was always boiling with jealousy, seeing me generally happy and light hearted at the stage of life she was struggling in. It makes sense now that she always hated it every time she found anything good about me at all. I was still the happy girl that I've been, even when I was just relaxing at home, and even with all that she was demanding for me to do. It appears that she couldn't relate to my positive energy and she hated it. She couldn't even understand it.

Was that her only problem, though? I couldn't be sure yet.

I figured that being married to Adam's father was probably one of the greatest accomplishments she had in her social life. Another accomplishment had to be that Adam was her son. Her family always said that Adam looked exactly like his father. It was no wonder that she always seemed to be clinging on to Adam, rather than allowing him to live normally. I've had many only child friends with single mothers, and their mothers were never as obsessive as Khatijah ever was. They may have been attentive, but not obsessive. My only child friends were allowed freedom and growth, with support for what they wanted to do. They're all relatively successful and independent.

Adam also once told me that Khatijah got married to a local Malay guy at first, and then she got divorced. Khatijah told him that her ex husband was too strict. It's odd, considering she has been nothing but extremely strict with me. She seemed to have been psychologically projecting her entire unfortunate past that she failed to cope with, on to me. It's a negative defense mechanism. There are many ways to survive, but she chose a negative one. It was her choice.

18

FINAL WARNING

It was 2016. It was the ending of our second year together. I had just performed an afternoon prayer. Adam didn't go to work. He came in the room with our dried laundry, crumpled up in his hands.

"Why do you have the laundry?" I asked him, while removing the top part of my prayer hijab.

"The maid's here," he said.

The maid was already there for a while and was about to be done soon.

"So why can't they be downstairs?" I asked, wondering why it was different that day. We all normally had our laundries still drying downstairs when the maid was there. If I only washed Adam's clothes, the maid was instructed to fold them.

"They're dry," he answered. He was already in a bad mood.

"No, why couldn't they be left downstairs so that I can fold them in the laundry room?" I asked him. "Now they're crumpled," I pointed out to him with disappointment.

"Whatever," he said, and dumped the clothes on the unmade bed. He left the room.

I felt so upset with him for not even being able to answer me properly. I quickly folded all the clothes and hung them up. I wasn't even in the mood for laundry. He came back in the room.

I nagged at him like he never left, "You couldn't even give me an answer. You just decided to crumple up the laundry, and force me to fold them. Why couldn't I just fold them in the laundry room?"

He walked back and forth in front of the bed when I was talking. And when I got done, he headed towards me in anger. He was just as monstrous as ever, only worse, because he had grown out his hair at the time. He looked more and more like a giant monster that couldn't tame his big, puffy, unkempt hair. It felt like a horror story. He raged against me with his hair shaking everywhere. I didn't want to get trapped against the wall again like the time he couldn't stop slamming me.

I jumped on the bed at the same time before it could happen, and we started wrestling each other. He wasn't beating me. I managed to use up some wrestling skills I got from when I was a kid, watching wrestling shows with my brothers and wrestling with them. I tricked my way out of his moves. I ended up locking his head in between my legs and I pulled his big hair. I was finally able to hurt him back. I pulled some of it out in my palms completely while he was on top of me. A chunk of his hair was in my hand, just as how I had a chunk of my hair in my hand that day at my mom's from being stressed with him. He screamed for me stop. He started crying. We stopped the match.

"You *know* I'm growing my hair out!" he cried to me. He was still on me, in between my legs.

I looked at him with a blank expression. I wondered what that's supposed to mean. Was there supposed to be rules for me to defend myself? Even if I had killed him right then with his hair all bald, it would have been my right to self-defense, wouldn't it?

"I've been trying to make it better," he said, looking at me with such sadness. He was still on me.

I actually did immediately feel bad. I remembered good times we had together when I gave him some at-home hair treatments. I always liked giving people beauty treatments and makeovers. I especially liked to give them to Adam, whatever spa treatments he wanted, but he never really asked for them.

I let go of my leg grip slowly while I was recalling.

As soon as he was released, he started beating me and couldn't let me go. I tried to fight back by wrestling again. It was still an unfair match, and it was still quite impossible to free myself out of his grips. He emotionally manipulated me with the hair thing.

I managed to reach out for his hair again and pulled it. The same thing happened.

"Stop!!!" he cried out. We stopped again. He really cried.

Then he grabbed me and pinned me down to the edge of the bed. It was the same position he choked me in every time in the room.

The last time he did this, he had me locked in the position, then he dug his elbows deep into my eye socket and I thought my head was going to break right then or my eyes would pop and I would die regardless. He held it there for a while and then let go of me. My eyes clearly became different in size after. One was swollen and the other one looked like it shrunk. I thought it was permanently going to be that way. Like the standard procedure, Adam still wouldn't let me see a doctor. He made sure of it.

This time, Adam locked me down with his body, pinning my head down with his right hand, putting the pressure of his bodyweight on my head. He started choking me with his left hand. Needless to say, I couldn't breathe. Once again, I thought I was going to die that way. I prepared myself to go. As annoying as I had to keep accepting my death that way, I really just had to. I had no choice. Not long enough for me to die, he let go of the choke, and he got up from putting pressure on my head.

Adam leaned back on the headboard to rest with his eyes closed, like nothing happened. I grabbed my phone and quickly took a photo of my neck that had blood marks on it, from the choke he gave me. I sent it to my family. It was the first time ever that I shared a photo of what Adam has been doing to me. Other parts of my body were also with blood marks, but I didn't need to send the photos.

My mom called the cops. She never liked me being with Adam anyway, from all the problems he was persistent to have with us. It was also the first time for my brothers to ever hear about it, too. None of them like him since then. It wasn't easy to reveal, as silly as it sounds. I knew that this was the first thing I should've done from the beginning. But it's definitely a lot easier said than done.

I never saw Adam as the dangerous man that all the psychologists and lawyers in the world could ever tell me he was. He was just my husband. Even after opening up to my family, I still wasn't able to open up to my friends, or anyone else. It was still difficult to.

Not long after, Khatijah knocked on the door.

Adam answered.

"The police are here and they're looking for you," she said to him, while pointing at him. She was monotone with her speech and body language, like she wasn't sure if it was really happening. She was so anxious, her face was all red. She was most likely worried that Adam would get locked up and that the neighbors would know the truth of how they were at home.

I immediately got up, too. I was surprised we didn't even hear the bell ring when we were so quiet in the room.

Adam looked like he got a minor heart attack while keeping his cool. He was too shocked to respond. He had a serious expression on his face.

"The police are here and they're looking for you," Khatijah repeated herself the same way to Adam, while pointing to him, and walking towards the stairs as we were all heading downstairs. While walking, she was watching Adam's face for his response.

I didn't put on my headscarf. I had a short sleeve top on, and I still had my maxi skirt on from my prayers that I didn't get the chance to change out of. When we got downstairs to the opened front door, I immediately felt Adam shaking through his energy and his breathing.

Three police officers were standing at the front door, looking all strong and guarded with their big guns, rifles, and shotguns. One of them was dressed in army camo with a matching hat and boots. He was just at the side, most likely for backup. One of the neighborhood guards also came. All four of the men were shocked to see the marks Adam left on me.

Adam and I stepped outside to talk to them, right in front of the door. Khatijah was standing at the door, holding on to the side. They took down our details for the record. I almost didn't give anyone the chance to talk, the moment I saw them. I was talking non-stop to them immediately, as if someone had asked me questions. I told them all that Adam did to me that day. Adam was trying his best to defend himself once in awhile, slowly moving back into the house to be at the other side of the door, next to Khatijah. I was the only one standing outside with the witnesses.

Khatijah was blurting out random things to us, interrupting us when we were talking to the cops at random times.

"Anyway, why don't you go out?" she tapped my left arm to get my attention, and randomly asked me. "Why do you act imprisoned?"

It seemed like she was trying to manipulate the situation, as if I ever had a problem with my living situation and that I was creating problems about it. Also, it was as though she was implying that I started a fight about being unhappy to live there. Clearly, it was not me, but Khatijah that wanted us to accompany her, but yet didn't want to share the living space with me at the same time. And, it was as if she never stopped me from going out, which she always did try hard to manipulate anyway, by making me feel uncomfortable.

I looked at Khatijah but I ignored her shameless desperation.

She was trying her best to distract the topic from abuse to any other random things possible she could come up with. But the cops, too, were too smart and focused to entertain her. It was clearly none of her business, especially when she surely couldn't care less about my condition. The condition of an abused young woman, who was also her daughter-in-law. Not once did she feel bad for my marks at all, just as how she ignored the marks all over me throughout the years.

"I already told you to move out!" she randomly said to Adam, once again, still trying to be heard by anyone.

Adam actually answered her, most likely because he was so anxious too anyway, and said, "Give me some time!"

It was a random issue that the cops weren't even there for, but it became our next plan together anyway. It got us secure in following through the plan of moving out. We did think about it before anyway, when Khatijah kept telling me to get my own kitchen.

The neighborhood guard was video recording everything on his phone, from the start.

When Khatijah realized it, she held one arm out to stop him from a distance, and told him, "No, don't record us..."

"It's just for reference later," the guard said, and he continued to record us. He was smart.

I was glad he did that. I wasn't scared at all, because it was really only better for me. If Khatijah didn't like it, then she should have left the scene that never needed her anyway.

I invited the cops to come into the house to see the condition of the bedroom, to prove to them of how Adam and Khatijah have always been, even before I came into their lives. They didn't accept nor did they reject the invitation. They were just listening and watching me, as I continued talking to them.

One cop that looked like the oldest, said, "Even though this is a problem between husband and wife, he's definitely in the wrong." He pointed to Adam and slightly nodded.

"How do you know he's wrong?" Khatijah asked.

"We can see the marks. Witnessing it is enough," he answered, looking at me.

The other cops were also agreeing with him at the same time, nodded and looked at me, "Yeah, the marks are enough to know."

Adam still tried to defend himself despite that.

"You don't know what she does to me. You don't know her mouth," he told them. "She hit me first," he continued.

"How does it make sense that a small girl like me with no fat, and no muscles, can hurt you? How does it make sense that I would take the risk, too? Prove it! Show a single mark on you," I suggested. He had nothing to show.

I immediately got distracted by how hot the younger cop was. He had the nicest body. He stepped forward to Adam like a boss to look at him one-on-one in the face. Would I be blamed for being attracted to another man that's just obviously better? All the men seemed so protective just by standing there, so much more than Adam ever was to me.

"You can come with us to file a report," the older one said to me.

"Where? Now?" I asked them.

"Yeah, now at the station," the hot one said. One by one, they were turning around to walk away slowly, for me to follow them.

"Wait! Let me talk to you," Adam said.

We all looked at him.

"I need to talk to you first," he said, looking at me.

"Okay, what?" I asked him. I wanted him to talk about it in front of everyone.

"Come here," he called me to come closer to him. He was ushering me in the house with him.

"Okay wait," I told the cops.

They waited for me, and Khatijah continued talking to them.

He ushered us into the laundry room where it was as private as we could get downstairs, and he started begging me to not make the police report.

"No," I said.

He kept trying and holding me so I wouldn't leave the room.

"No," I still said.

He started crying so much.

"Please, I promise I'll be better for you... I'll get us a new place and everything will be better... Please. I promise I'll be a better man. I promise I'll give you anything you want," he cried. "I'm sorry, I promise I won't hurt you anymore..." he said.

He was shaking. His every breath, and every cell on his body seemed like they were vibrating.

I didn't feel love for him, but when I heard the apology, I had to think about it. I always believed that it's wrong to reject apologies. So as annoying as it is that I did so, I chose to forgive him again. Spiritually, I felt I had to. I falsely believed I had to continue respecting him as my husband, even in such circumstance. Whether he was honest with me or not, I thought, I couldn't be sure until later.

We went back to the cops at the front door. Khatijah was still standing at the side of the door, talking to them about things they probably weren't entertaining.

"It's okay," I told the cops. I held out my right hand and nodded at them with a slight smile.

They looked surprised and asked, "Yeah?"

"Yeah, it's okay now, thank you so much," I told them. I slightly smiled at them, to convince them that I was happy, in order to protect Adam. Even though I wasn't happy at all. "You'll still have all the details, right?" I asked the older cop, just in case.

"Yeah," he said. He showed me the stapled papers he was holding, where our names were. "So if anything happens, you just call us again," he assured me. The other cops nodded at me in assurance, too. They probably thought I was so innocent to do that, by the way they were, but we all knew they didn't have rights to intrude. I've made my decision.

"Thank you so much," I said to them.

As the cops were leaving, the neighborhood guard asked to talk to Adam. They had a talk outside the house. The guards were always friendly with the neighborhood. I had a feeling he was giving Adam some advice on marriage.

Meanwhile, my mom called Khatijah and told her to have a talk with Adam about divorcing me. All Khatijah said in response was, "They're always fighting!"

She had her desperate, whining expression, of course.

I was glad my mom didn't have to see that annoying expression.

I walked from the living room to the dining room, where she was.

Khatijah got off the phone at the same time, went to the living room, and started organizing some pillows. She was avoiding talking to me and even looking at me. I still never got any worries from her for what Adam did to me. The cops' reactions were much more nurturing than she ever was in the entire two years.

I watched her from the dining room, while she was ignoring that I was there.

Adam came in the house eventually, and asked, "How did they get in?"

"I left the gates opened because I was expecting someone," Khatijah said. "How did they get here?" she asked.

"I don't know," Adam said.

My brothers wanted me to leave Adam. They, including my mom, were disappointed with me when they heard that I chose to continue with him. My older brother Ace called Adam to warn him. Like the rest of my brothers, it was the first time Ace heard about it. He would get involved in our problems if Adam hurt me again. Ace was a college football player in Texas, and he's also experienced with fights. He even beat up the school bully, at least twice his size, for messing with me on the school bus before. There was blood. Everyone enjoyed watching it.

I rested for a month at home to heal, and while I searched for a new place with Adam. We weighed down all our options. We decided on a rental apartment about five minutes away, on the same road. It didn't matter to me where it was going to be. I was just willing to give the man I was married to, the chance that he was asking for.

19

THIRD TIME'S A CHARM

It was the beginning of our third year together. Our final year together. Having Khatijah out of our daily presence felt so fresh. Adam and I no longer had anyone constantly bothering us throughout the day. We had so much fun living the way we wanted to, and doing things the way we were comfortable with doing. It was the best thing that ever happened to us in our entire marriage experience. Adam was no longer giving me random attacks at all, either. We were more at peace, and we were able to spend more time together at home with no interruptions.

What I loved about the apartment was that it was very affordable. The entire unit of three plus one bedrooms, with two bathrooms, was around the price of a single studio room I normally would rent. I was sure the price was good, even for the location. It was next to a forest reserve, blocking out a lot of the sounds of traffic. We always had fresh air there, too. Most of the time it was cooling enough that Adam rarely needed to use the air conditioner. I rarely ever needed the air conditioner, anyway. A few times, I was freezing in the morning with just the fan on. It was a low-rise apartment. Adam hated high-rise buildings, so the place felt meant for us. During the day, monkeys and baboons had meals in the apartment trash bin. They ran around the walls of the apartment compound that separated the forest, and they hung around the trees with their babies. They looked scary sometimes, but they were adorably shy. They amused me a lot.

Despite all the changes, however, Adam's short temper was still obviously there. One day during dinner at home, I told him about how much I appreciated a high-end, luxury fashion designer, Roberto Cavalli. I appreciated his workmanship a lot.

"I really like Roberto Cavalli. He's so good," I told Adam. I visited Roberto Cavalli's website on my phone.

Before I could continue on to talk more about it, or to even show him anything on my phone, Adam quickly said, "He's not even a Muslim. And you wanna support him."

I didn't understand that, so I defended my appreciation, regardless.

"Oh, I have no worries about that," I answered.

He couldn't take it, so much that he got up from eating with me, and started walking around the living room, yelling out random things at me. He was constantly repeating the designer's name while telling me to shut up, in an angry, mocking tone. He was telling me to shut up, while as if the designer's name was my name.

"Shut up, Roberto Cavalli! Shut up, Roberto Cavalli..! Shut up, Roberto Cavalli..!" He was being so loud. He couldn't stop repeating the same things, non-stop. His voice was echoing, bouncing on the empty walls that were waiting to display my decorations. We had loud music on before, but never that loud.

I wasn't even saying anything to him. He just went on chanting, like the time I recorded him chanting gibberish and he ended up choking me in the end.

He was worrying me. I hurried closer to him to calm him down. I tried my best to get him to stop, but he wouldn't. I got tired of him walking around me in a circle while chanting, so I sat down on the floor next to the sofa, on a bamboo rug. I watched him in his hysteria. I wondered why God wanted me to experience this. I knew that Adam hated talking about fashion in general, but he didn't have to be so disturbed about it to this extent every single time. I literally didn't even get the chance to talk about the designer at all. I didn't even ask him to buy me anything. All I said was that I liked him and that I appreciated his work. That was it. I answered back to Adam's irrational yelling, ignoring his foolish ways to control me.

"I still like the designer!" I told him.

He still responded the same way, and he still continued on with his hysteria.

"I still don't see a problem with it," I told him, still not understanding his problem.

He was still the same, walking around in circles, around me. It was scary, and it felt like I was talking to myself. I wished he was more rational and level-headed.

He grabbed two scissors on the floor that he had left from a DIY project we were working on for the windows. He raised them up to his head like a slasher-type killer, and immediately charged towards me with them in anger while stomping his feet, about to stab me. When he got to me, he continued with the motion of stabbing me, but he didn't do it. It was so close.

I continued sitting on the bamboo rug where I was, unmoved. I didn't believe he was going to do it, although at the back of my mind I knew it was still possible. I knew his irrational temper, and I was well aware of what I had gone through for the past two years plus. I still waited on the rug where I was, till he walked away and dropped the scissors. I took note of where they were. He went back to the dining area and I slowly followed him.

"Please stop this," I told him.

He answered back by grabbing the vacuum my mom gave us, and threw it at me. It was in the dining area because I had just vacuumed all our shoes at the entrance and I left it there. The entrance was just about two to three meters away from us. I quickly blocked myself when he threw it at me. The vacuum fell with some parts of it disassembled. I was shocked he did that. Adam probably knew he was starting to hurt me again and that he could get in trouble, so he ran out of the house. He was too afraid to beat me up anymore because of the police and my brother. He was aware enough of the situation, that he was looking for other alternatives to hurt me.

I quickly told my family what happened. My younger brother Razz came to pick me up to leave Adam for good, and to stay at my mom's. I was so speechless all the way to my mom's, bothered by how Adam could be that way. Whatever happened to him for him to end up like this, must have really cracked him up in the head. I needed to know why, why was he like that?

Razz was lecturing me about leaving him. Meanwhile, Ace immediately called Adam to have a word with him. I didn't know what was said, but Adam refrained from hurting me again for many months more. Because yes, I went back to the house after a few days and I continued to stay with him.

Adam was intimidated by Ace, so much that he would sometimes randomly bring him up, as if Ace had done anything wrong to him. He was so bitter that Ace was able to warn him, and was able to protect me against him. He was bitter he didn't have total control over me. It shocked me so much that he had deep issues to the point of hating his own brother-in-law who has been nothing but decent with him. He also implied that Ace was just being a slave of money, because he was in the corporate world.

Twice, when we were still staying at his mom's, I told Adam that Ace would beat him up for abusing me. He told me to go ahead and bring him, because he would kill Ace. He was very serious about me understanding that every time. I knew how deliberately vicious Adam can be, so I never wanted to ask for help from my brother. He made it clear that he would really kill him.

I didn't realize how unreasonable it was until Nate helped me see it clearly. If Adam was really brave enough to fight against my brother, he wouldn't need to threaten me about anything. I guess my protective instincts just felt like my brother had to be protected and kept away from Adam. Even though Ace could definitely knock him out with no help. He can independently fight against unreasonable men, unlike Adam, who was a wife beater, and always needed lots of people to back him up in life and to even control me.

I was enjoying our peace since the last outburst. I wanted to discuss with him about work. It was after we just had dinner, hanging out at the dining table.

"I think I should vlog," I said to him, thinking of what I could do that's not a nine-to-five. Then I got excited with an idea and said, "And I can continue my studies! I'm so excited…! I can do my Masters in Islamic Studies! It can be done in like, two years!"

"You have to go a long way if you want to be like the scholars though," he said to me.

"No, really, it can be done in two years," I said to him.

"Yeah, but if you wanna be like the scholars then you have to take years. You think the scholars had it so easy? They spent a long time to get to where they are," he told me.

"No… it depends on how long you take. Some can take six years, while some can just spend two years on it," I told him. "If I focus on it, I can be done quick," I added.

"You think you can be like the scholars…" he said to me.

"What?" I asked him. "No one's perfect," I said.

"Whatever, scholar," he mocked again.

"Why are you so jealous?" I asked in confusion.

"Shut up, scholar," he said to me.

"Oh my gosh… what's wrong with you? You can't even be happy for me at all?"

He got up to go to our home office and shut the door. I followed him and tried to open the locked door. I knocked on the door.

"Open the door," I said.

"Shut up, scholar," he said.

"I wanna help you through whatever you wanna do, too! Why can't you be happy for me? Why can't you see that it's our success together?" I asked him. I always offered him suggestions and help for his businesses, even though he never wanted to accept them.

He was silent, and then he continued, "Scholar!"

Then I got so pissed off with him.

"Look, I know you're jealous of me. But that's not my fault you can't deal with it. Not my fault you don't wanna focus on your life," I told him.

"Shut up, scholar!" he started yelling.

"Yes, okay, I'm a scholar!" I yelled back. "Open the door! I'm not your mom, I'm not gonna be banging on the door."

"Shut up, scholar! Vlogger!"

"Oh my gosh, why are you so jealous?!" I asked him, so confused with the surreal dimension I was in.

"Scholar...!" he yelled again so childishly.

"Let's just get a divorce," I said, with disappointment.

He laughed and said, "And you want to be a scholar?"

"So...? Divorce is not a sin...?" I told him. How does it make sense that to be a religious scholar, one has to be divorce-free? Islam was meant to be realistic, not judgmental.

He continued laughing to himself.

"Why don't you just divorce me and get all this over with. Would you divorce me if I give you ten thousand ringgits? Think about it," I suggested.

There was silence.

"I'll give you ten thousand ringgits," I repeated myself.

Then I heard a loud thud on the door that surprised me.

I knew he punched it.

"Open the door!" I called out to him. I knocked on the door with my palms and turned the knob fast repeatedly.

He ignored me.

I got tired of everything so I went to the bedroom to have some peace of mind. I left him alone to calm down, and I fell asleep.

I woke up later and saw that he had already opened the office door. He was getting ready to leave the house for some late night meetings.

The next day, I sat in the office with him. Him on his computer, while I was on my laptop. I was finally able to talk about what I could do, with him. He was accepting them, but with restrictions. There was so much I had to be careful about, to the point of me having to be sure that only females can watch my vlogs. I thought it was quite ridiculous and unrealistic, but I agreed just because I wanted to at least have something to do, anything at all.

Then I looked at the hole he punched on the door.

"Okay. And you know the landlord's gonna keep the deposit if they see the door, right?" I reminded him.

"Yeah, I'm getting it fixed anyway," he said.

"How? You can find the exact door?" I asked.

"Yeah, should be fine," he said, calmly. He was happy with my agreement, and happy in general.

Keeping Adam sane and stable felt like a task I had, every day that I was with him. Studying his reactions to new factors, and obtaining data from it. He was a major research project. A case study.

One beautiful day, we went to his cousin's wedding. Everything was going very well. However, as expected, Mak Rubi, the one who shamelessly told me to stay away from Adam for months, did her usual nosy duty there.

The wedding was in a medium sized multipurpose hall in a mall. Adam and I stood in the buffet line for our lunch.

"Hi, Assalamualaikum, Mak Rubi!" I greeted her cheerfully in Arabic.

"Walaikumsalam," she answered.

She started shaking slightly but she was focused on talking to Adam.

This time, she told him, "Invite your mom to your new place."

Why was it any of her concern? Again, I don't even know.

"Yeah, we will!" I happily told her.

She ignored me. She was watching Adam's reaction.

Adam was never interested in having any of his controlling, judgmental family members at the apartment, so he just laughed. He used his charms as usual, to shut her up.

"It's not a very nice place," he said. Although Adam and I loved the place. We often talked about how perfect it was for us.

"Oh, it's okay, just invite her," Mak Rubi said, with her face lit up looking at Adam.

"No, it's okay, it's not a very nice place," he repeated himself, laughing about it and flashing his smile.

"It doesn't matter, just let her go to your place," she still insisted. She couldn't even take the simple hint.

Adam and I both had no response to her as we reached our turn for the buffet. We then got interrupted by another cousin of Adam's who was taking photographs for the wedding. The three of us took a photo together and we ended our conversation.

Since we settled into our apartment, I talked about having our families over a lot, for them to see our place. I was so excited, I even planned to have both our moms visit us first, after we would have lunch somewhere on a regular day with them. Then, both of our relatives would visit us separately over a holiday or special occasion. I even specifically wanted Adam's aunt, Maklong, and her husband, Paklong, and her daughter who was Adam's older cousin, to come over one day, too. The three of them were my favorite people in his mom's side of the family. They were probably the sanest and decent ones I met, amongst a few others I could count with one hand.

Adam was never thrilled by any of the suggestions. He always just looked at me with no reactions at all to them. I should be the one that knew Adam best, for being his wife, but Mak Rubi seemed to have her head in the clouds, thinking she had any rights to intrude again. It's highly likely that she was jealous seeing us happy, as it seemed like she was, since ever. Even if we never invited anyone at all, that would have still been none of her concern. Regardless, I remained patient with her lack of decency and social etiquette, and I continued being nice to her.

It was odd, though, that she has a daughter who always seemed to follow her grumpy expressions, and almost as if she would be ready to play rugby and attack someone. She was always like this unless she were to take photos. She was the one daughter of Mak Rubi amongst three daughters, in her thirties, who never experienced marriage before but really wanted to, to the point of always being a side girl to someone already taken. The guy clearly couldn't commit to her, but she was still trying to be with him, according to Adam and Khatijah. She had to cancel her wedding a few times, and she still wanted him. I wondered why Mak Rubi raised her daughter with such low dignity, while obsessing so much about me and Adam. It was also very observable that even Mak Rubi's husband seemed to be so speechless all the time, even when they were the hosts of some family gatherings. She clearly had some personal things to work on herself and her awkward family, but instead, she was neglecting her own life in order to consistently disrespect mine and my husband's personal life more. It was irrational and outrageously disgraceful of her.

Adam and I sat at our table with our food.

"Baby. Mak Rubi was so annoying," I told him.

He answered with such gentleness to me, and said, "I know, baby, she's annoying… she's always annoying. But don't let any of the annoying women with nothing better to do, bother you. Just forget about it, okay?"

"I know…" I answered, disappointed with people's inability to be kind and loving. I looked around wondering how people can be so horrible.

We finished eating, and we went to the waiting room where the other relatives were. There was a break for the wedding reception that was planned to be held after.

All of a sudden, an old man, a relative of Adam's, suddenly came forward to me.

"I heard there's going to be a gathering at your place!" he looked at me with a mischievous expression.

I was offended by that expression. I knew this old man. I always entertained him every time I saw him. He was charming with my mom once during an Eid al-Fitr celebration, too, that I helped Khatijah host and cook.

"What?" I asked him, showing him that I was offended.

"I heard Adam invited everyone!" he told me, still with the same mischievous old man expression. Then I immediately knew gossip happened while we were eating. I also immediately had a feeling Mak Rubi was spiteful enough to imply or spread around a lie.

Adam was with me the entire time, and he still was. I looked at Adam wondering what was meant, and he was surprised, too.

"No," I said to him sternly as I looked at the old man in his mischievous eyes. "He never did. Even if there was an invitation, it was from me. Adam didn't invite anyone," I told him sternly.

It was about time the family learned to shut their mouths to learn some facts first. The entire waiting room of Adam's loud relatives got quiet when I was saying that, and for a few more seconds after until they gradually went back to normal.

The old man never bothered me with gossip anymore, and I was quite glad he blurted it out to me. We continued being just fine after, as we were before he gave me that expression. He didn't take it personally. His wife was there too, and she was always nice to me, regardless. They always seemed to be at peace, undisturbed by others.

Adam didn't like what happened. He rarely ever liked sharing blunt truths other than with me, while I was always quite notorious for being forthright with everyone. It helps make people more intelligent, and that makes for a better world, to me.

Adam walked out of the waiting room and I followed behind him.

"Where are we going?" I asked him.

"We're leaving," he said. We were already outside the hall, still walking.

"No, why?" I got confused.

So what if people can't handle me? Ain't that one of their many problems? It's not like I was rude. I treated everyone equally, and if anyone wanted answers from me, they got it. They received honest, straightforward answers from me, with no hidden agendas. Unlike what I was receiving back at the wedding.

We stopped in front of the escalator. It was very bright and clear. Still a very beautiful day. We were right in front of an opened glass door to a balcony. There were some boys hanging out on the balcony about three metres away from us, talking and having their cigarettes. I could see them through the rest of the glass walls. I didn't like the cigarette smell.

"Why did you have to answer like that?" he asked me, referring to the old man scene.

"What do you mean? What's wrong with what I did?" I asked him. "Oh, I see… you just wanna look good all the time to everyone, dontchu? Even if they're lies?"

"Fuck what people think. You think I give a shit about any of them?" he said.

"Then what's the problem with what I did?" I asked.

He was silent. We were silent for a while, standing there doing nothing. Ultimately, I didn't care what his choice was going to be.

"We're leaving," he said again and walked down the escalator. I followed him. I didn't care about being there anymore either. Why should I, after being blamed for no reason?

Instead of walking down all the way to the ground floor to exit the mall, he decided to stop on the first floor, and walked all the way back behind the elevators, to where there was nothing. It was an empty part of the mall that was still under construction. He stopped in front of an elevated wooden platform that looked like a small corner stage. We sat on it.

I was so frustrated that we had to do all the stupid emotional things when we could have just continued to have fun.

"What are we doing?" I asked him. "I thought we were leaving."

He asked me, "Why can't you just ignore them?"

"Why should I? Why don't you ask *them* to ignore us? Why are they so obsessed with us?" I asked him. I was getting so pissed off with him. "You're blaming *me* for everything that happened? You couldn't even be honest about our place. You had to lie. At least I was honest. It would've been better if you could be honest and just tell Mak Rubi off. Who gives a shit if we look bad? Who's the one that started it? How much longer do we have to get annoyed with that stupid fucked up bitch? How many more lies are we gonna tell to shut her up?"

He couldn't answer me. Maybe he was embarrassed with his family all that while and he just didn't know how to express it. Blaming me was a lot easier for his ego. I didn't want to have to get there, but he was asking for it. He couldn't just use his common sense and be logical about things. He couldn't be brave. Even with his own family. He walked off immediately and used the escalator at the back where we were, that wasn't running. I didn't realize it till I got there. I was wearing heels. He ran off so fast, I didn't know where he was anymore by the time I got to the escalator. Screw it, I thought. I walked down the escalator anyway.

I called him.

"Where are you?" I asked.

"I'm at the car," he said.

I got to the car that was parked right in front of the entrance of the mall. I got in the car and I buckled myself up, ready to go.

"Can you start the engine?" I asked him. It seemed like he was only testing me. He thought I didn't want to leave. He looked like he was surprised I said that.

"Let's go back in," he said.

"Why?" I asked him, not really caring.

"I feel better now. Let's go back," he said.

"Oh it's okay then, I'll wait for you here," I said. No way I just spent all that time walking around like the abandoned wife that I was, only to walk back in, acting like everything was fine.

"Let's just go," he said. He got out of the car with the keys.

I still didn't care. I wasn't going back to the circus, wasting the beautiful day. I started waiting for him patiently, having a marvelous time in the car with the soft sun shining on me. I opened the door for some air that was clear with wind. It was so relaxing.

Adam came back in the car. He started the engine.

"What happened?" I asked him.

"I don't wanna go anymore," he said.

I shut my door.

We left the wedding for good and it continued to be peaceful. I remember the feeling so clearly. I was secretly so happy. As we were leaving, it immediately felt refreshing. It felt good that he didn't harm me, and that he was also following how I felt for once. I had tears in my eyes. I appreciated it so much.

Finally, I felt some hope in Adam's behavior, that I even decided to stop taking birth control pills. I was on the pills for a while, since our second year together. I thought I should finally accept the possibility of having children with him. I was always afraid to, as it would mean that I would be stuck with him somehow, no matter what.

After skipping the next pill that I was supposed to take, I had pregnancy symptoms. I had no period for three months. We went for two checkups for the first two months, but they were negative each time. I took a home pregnancy test for the third month, and it was negative, as well. I learned that it was normal for my hormones to get confused after withdrawal. When I got my period again after the three months, I accepted that I was not pregnant, and I confirmed it with Adam.

He suddenly started behaving rude to me again, like all the peaceful times never happened. I childishly thought of continuing his patience by acting like I still felt pregnant, even with my period. I even bloated up my stomach to show him, even though it was still flat when I didn't do anything.

He kept asking me, "Where? There's no fat! Look at mine!"

I answered him, "We're the same!"

It worked, but only for a few months. I was actually believing it, too, from some research I did on odd pregnancies. Adam got tired of buying me home pregnancy tests and seeing them all negative. I asked him to take me to one more checkup, and he didn't want to. He couldn't believe it anymore.

I knew why I thought I was ready to accept a baby. I really wasn't, actually. It was only because I was at a point where I had nothing else to do at all other than take care of Adam every day. I was glad I wasn't pregnant, because I read that abusive men would even hurt the baby. They also wouldn't care at all to abuse their wives in front of their children, too. Privately, they pretty much only care about themselves.

20

THE SLAVE REVOLT

It was January, 2017. The ending of our third year together. Khatijah was going for a one-month holiday with her cousin. Adam had to drop her off at the airport, and he asked me to follow him. He said that we would go for dinner afterwards. I thought it was so sweet of him, so I quickly prepared myself for a beautiful night together. We picked his mom up, and we went on our way to the airport.

As anticipated, Khatijah wouldn't say a single word to me, unless she wanted to be rude. As usual, she was having conversations with Adam alone, about things that only Adam would know about, such as her errands that he would normally have to do for her. It never bothered me. I always kept myself occupied somehow at the back. I would either check myself out in my pocket mirror or use my phone. I was always fine like that.

Then all of a sudden, Khatijah turned around and asked me in a very offensive way, "Still not working?"

I was shocked by her sudden rudeness, considering both her and her son have been oppressing me from work. Apart from that, in Islam, it is the woman's choice whether she wants to work or not. It's never a responsibility, if she's married. However, as it was also anticipated for Khatijah to do that, I still chose to be patient with her.

I nicely answered with a laugh, "Do I have to work?"

She was surprised by my answer. She paused for a while, unable to answer my question in return.

Then instead, she mindlessly said, "I'm just playing around, don't be so sensitive."

Her answer just didn't make sense to how the conversation was flowing. It was clear to me then that she wanted to manipulate the conversation as if I had responded sensitively, even when I was so patient with her, and wanting more peace as always. It seemed as though she planned to approach me rudely in a way that would only allow her to imply that I was sensitive in the end. She was willing to make it appear that way, even if my answer still didn't match up to how she wanted the outcome to be.

Also, I took note of how she has given me the same exact answer many times before. They were in the same exact way, and also in the car, when we would be driving somewhere. It was always disgustingly insensitive, and it seemed as though she thought it was a good scene to keep repeating. But there we were again, I chose to be patient with her.

We finally dropped Khatijah off kindly at the airport.

Then as we headed for dinner, I asked Adam, "Where are we going, exactly? Where are we having dinner?"

"We're going to my friend's place first to pick up some drugs, and then dinner," he answered.

"What? How come you never told me? I don't wanna be a part of this," I said. I was so shocked, because I had no idea we were picking up drugs.

"I already told you," he said. This was always his answer if I ever didn't agree to something.

"No, you didn't. Now you're forcing me to go with you, and I don't want that," I said, "I just wanna eat, I'm hungry."

"It's too late, we're already almost there," he scolded me. "Why do you think we're having dinner in this area? Why do you think I'm going to spend at a nice cafe for you instead of any other cheap place, if we're not stopping by my friend's?!"

I was so hurt. "I thought it was near the airport," I said.

"No, it's not!" he answered back, shouting.

"You like the cafe, and you wanna go there," I said with another answer. "But if it's such a burden to pay for me then I'll pay. Sorry you have to pay for me."

He continued shouting at me so loud, like he was out in a battle field, while saying, "I don't care! I want to have dinner! I'm hungry!"

"It's still a bad night now anyway. You didn't tell me you're getting drugs, and you don't even really wanna have a nice dinner. I'm hungry too, and I said I don't wanna pick up the drugs. And your mom was so rude, asking me about work again when she knows she oppressed me to begin with," I said calmly, while feeling sad. "I should've asked her, 'still not a nice person yet'?"

"Yes, good! You should've! Tell her then! Why didn't you ask her?!"

"I will then! Next time!" I shouted back at him, mirroring him.

He started slamming on the steering wheel with his hands while saying, "Slave! Shut up, slave!"

"I *know* I'm a slave… a slave of God… And so are you, you're a slave of God, too," I said, not understanding why he has called me a slave a few times before.

It seemed like he didn't expect me to say that. He had a surprised pause.

"You're God's slave, and you're *my* slave!" he then yelled, giving me chills all over my arms and neck.

"Oh my gosh, are you serious? I'm not your slave… I'm no man's slave… Why are you so stupid?" I asked him sternly. I couldn't be any more serious with the question.

"It's the law, stupid! You don't even know the law! You don't know the law?! Stupid! Stupid! Stupid!" he repeated himself while yelling and slamming on the steering wheel simultaneously, like he wanted to kill his car. I couldn't believe how persistent he was to make me feel stupid. I was absolutely sure and I had faith that Islam was better than that. I never read oppressive or ugly verses before. They were always just misunderstood and gone wild in the media, or misinterpreted by people. I don't even consider anything uncomfortable as 'Islamic'. This so-called fact of the Syariah law made me feel very uncomfortable.

"That's not the law...?! Are you seriously stupid?!" I asked and yelled back. "Where? Where's the verse? Tell me which verse says that!"

He paused and scowled at me with annoyance, "Find it yourself, read!"

By this time, we passed the cafe that we were going to, and we got to his friend's place in just one minute. I was quiet while he continued yelling at me in the car even when he got out of the car to see his friend. He had no shame in treating me that way. He got back in the car and within the few minutes that we were almost at the cafe, I started crying to myself silently. When he parked the car, he didn't bother to comfort me at all. He got out and waited for me behind the car for about ten seconds. He walked to my side of the car and opened the door.

"Get out," he impatiently told me. He grabbed my phone away and watched me. I didn't care that he had my phone. He hurt me too much.

I silently and stubbornly didn't want to move, and I didn't even know if I could. I was in so much pain emotionally that I remained silent, and my tears kept falling even when I didn't know what to think of anymore. I was so hurt. I knew that he was wrong. I wondered how he learned this or even got this idea. Maybe he viewed his mother as his father's slave. Or every woman in general, as their husband's slaves, as he believed it was the law.

I've been patient with him all this while, genuinely, as his wife. I knew it would have been a completely different outcome if I had known that wife meant slave, to him. I would never have tolerated even a second of harm that he has ever given me, if I were his slave. I would never have felt sorry for all his crying, if I were his slave. I would never even want to have dinner with him after all that I had gone through to keep him happy, if I were his slave.

Instead of comforting me or waiting for me to feel better again, after less than a minute, he unbuckled my seat belt quickly and he started grabbing my arms with nothing but his fingernails, digging through my sleeves. I was forced to get out of the car as he tore the skin on my arms. My body tilted to follow his pull.

He let go, and more tears kept flowing out of my eyes.

"I would usually pinch you anyway," he said to me.

He was trying to make me believe that he was only 'pinching' me. He liked to pinch me on the arms while biting his lips a lot, to express that I'm adorable.

I shifted back to sit in the car properly.

Then he did it again.

He forced me to get out of the car by grabbing my arms with nothing but his fingernails, digging through my sleeves even harder this time.

As I was forced out of the car, I got on the sidewalk, and headed towards the road. I wanted to leave him for good.

He grabbed me and said, "Stop."

I was so disgusted. It was the sick cycle of hurting me and crying for me back, again.

"I want a divorce," I said, while walking away.

"No," he said, while holding me back, not allowing me to go anywhere. He hugged me tight to stop me from moving at all.

"Let me go," I told him.

"No, stop," he said.

"I need a divorce, let me go," I said, while still held tightly in his arms, unable to move. "Help!!!" I screamed.

"Shut up," he said.

"Help!!!" I screamed again. I continued to scream for people around to be aware of what he was doing to me and to help me. I saw some people outside the cafe. No one came. I didn't want to freak anyone out anyway either, actually.

He let go of me.

I started running away from him.

He caught up to me at the corner of the road, grabbed me again in the same way, picking me up in the air. My feet touched the ground and he held me still.

I tried moving around but I couldn't. I stretched out my arms as much as I could to reach his face. I grabbed his glasses off him and threw it to the side. I didn't want him to be so blind that he would need my help in the end, so I threw it gently to the side where the grass was. Instead of the drain.

He let go of me to look for his glasses on the grass, as I ran away crossing the road. I was turning around once in awhile to see what he was up to. I almost got distracted enough to get hit by some cars. He was already on his way, running towards me while crying. He looked so pathetic, I felt like throwing up. I had the worst feeling when I saw him running towards me like that. Who is this person? Why did I ever trust him? I was probably as naive, as naive could get. All I know now is that I've tried whatever I could as his wife. It was difficult, but I did persevere in the end.

I've reached the end of my wifehood for Adam. I couldn't see him as my husband anymore. He has finally crossed the ultimate limit, the very end of my patience. Even if he had pretended to kill himself, I wouldn't have bought it. He was too disturbing for me. I decided to head to the neighborhood mosque around the corner, as it was the safest place for me to go to. As I headed towards it, Adam caught up to me and started begging me to stop. I stopped to listen to what he had to say. He wanted me to just have dinner with him. I continued to reject him, then he continued crying even louder, wailing, and running away back towards the car. He went on a pathway through spacious land that looked like an empty park. There were clear, dim lights around the path way, for a romantic night stroll. Adam was stomping his feet while running, and letting his arms spread out by his side. It was just as awkward-looking as it sounds. It was the same way he would stomp his feet crying out of the bedroom before, only this time, I was watching him stomping away in a longer distance, under the dim lights. And it was in public. I couldn't believe how he seemed to not care that people could hear his wailings and see the way he was running. There was no one around in the path way, but anyone could have still seen that from a distance anyway. It was so hard to absorb, but it was truly happening right before me. I wondered why he reminded me of a toddler, crying, for not getting what he wanted. He could have been a cartoon character by the way he was behaving. It could have been a comedy. But it was really sad, and even more so, it was really scary.

I got to the mosque, but it took me awhile to get in. I didn't know that they would lock every single gate they had except for the main one that was facing the road. I had to walk around the entire mosque. When I finally got in, I checked my phone. It was on vibrate mode in my small leather sling bag. I had four missed calls from Adam, but I didn't feel the calls at all. Maybe my adrenaline was too high and I was too focused, walking non-stop. I didn't worry about the calls then, because I knew that if Adam wanted to apologize and to correct himself about the slavery, he knew where I was heading. There was nothing else around the area that I could have been heading to, but the mosque. There was nothing else around, after the mosque. Only a road back to the highway.

I spent quite a while there. I finally got some peace. I cooled myself off, freshened up, and took photos of the new marks. I was left a big, deep, purple bruise, bigger than my palms, surrounding the skin he tore on my arms. My other arm had red marks from his grip, too.

When I was done there, I gave Adam a call to get an update of where he was. He didn't answer. I walked all the way back to where the car was, and it wasn't there. I called him twice more. He answered and told me he wasn't in the area. I didn't bother with him anymore. I didn't even know why I still did. He only waited for a duration of four calls, while I was walking to the mosque. I couldn't even feel shocked anymore that he had no decency to at least worry about me, after all that he did to me. I felt nothing at all.

I walked up the stairs of the cafe. It was a very nice cafe, spacious, with variety of different types of seatings, and glass walls surrounding it. They had yellow lighting inside with their cafe name brightly lit at the entrance. I sat outside where I could secretly watch people watching me. Maybe some of them knew I was the crazy woman screaming earlier. I wasn't used to the area. People there are different. They're a lot more cultural than the areas in Malaysia I was used to. I felt them observing me for being a girl that was alone at night.

I focused on my phone. It was dying, at 12% battery life. Of all nights, God blessed me with driver apps that wouldn't work. I quickly messaged Nate whatever I could tell him of my situation before my phone died. I waited for his response while I reset my phone for the apps to work. I used the cafe's bathroom to wash up again and continued to sit inside at the corner. Nate never answered. Thursday night. He was probably sleeping. I forgot some people actually had work on week days.

My phone battery was getting lower, with the driver apps still unable to respond. There were no cabs around the spacious neighborhood. I wondered if I should hitchhike. I had the habit of hitchhiking before I got married. But I wasn't sure if I still wanted to do that.

But there I was at the cafe that night. I wasn't sure if I wanted to hitchhike anymore. All the men around me appeared to be typical Malay. Maybe they're all like Adam. I opened my contacts list in desperation. My eyes were quickly locked on Aaron, a man I dated before, for a month. I knew him for years as a good friend, and I even met his family who were always open-minded and friendly.

Aaron was also a good friend of Nate. He wrote to me a few weeks before to tell me he heard about me from Nate, and that he would be there for me, 'no matter what'. That made Aaron my first choice to get help from, but at the same time it made me feel guilty to. I was still thinking. My heart was beating fast in anxiety. I had a time limit to my decision. I was married, but I needed help. Adam spent a lot of time with random girls in his car at night for quick meetings, anyway. At least Aaron would be my hero for the night.

Screw the guy who called me his slave.

I had to give Aaron a try. I asked him, and he said he didn't mind. He didn't even ask me questions. He lived about an hour away from the area, but he was at a meeting at the time, which made him only half an hour away. I was in luck. I was so anxious to be seeing him again after years of silence. I was already there for three hours since I went to the mosque. Aaron got there at the perfect timing when my phone had reached 1% battery life, and then it died. Everything seemed to be in perfect timing for me to be seeing him that night.

I got in Aaron's truck with mocktails. I was so nervous, but I acted calm. He looked different from how he used to be. He gained some weight, looking better than before. He grew out his thick wavy hair and had it neatly tied back. He reminded me of a musician, and he did make music before anyway. He still looked masculine. I think he's taller than Adam.

"So what's going on?" he asked me, while he was driving away slowly from the cafe.

I started shaking and tears flew out my eyes uncontrollably. I was talking, but unclear, even to me. I can't remember what I was trying to say. I was so embarrassed. I cried a few times to Adam before, but he always made fun of it immediately and would even run away. Sick, right? It affected me so bad that I felt anxious to even cry with Aaron.

I saw Aaron slightly panicking, turning his head to look at me a few times while focusing on the road. It was so cute. I knew it's not easy for men to deal with women crying. At the same time, I had bad thoughts that he would do the same to me as Adam always did. I refused to express how sad I was really feeling inside. I chose to be happy, and I didn't want to talk about anything that had to do with Adam. I didn't want to feel sad.

Aaron didn't know the extent of the abuse Adam had done to

me, because I never once talked to him about it. I never even told Nate or Tina before. They didn't need to hear details. Hearing me abused was enough for them to know I was with an unstable man.

"Anyway, what about you?" I asked him, when I was done.

My mood swiftly went up to being happy with him.

I didn't think about it much at the time, but Aaron seemed to be quite concerned still. He had more seriousness to him than I was used to. I don't blame him. If I had seen myself then, I would probably be worried about me, too.

He was focused on finding a solution to keeping me safe, while I was focused on being happy. Two different conversations were happening simultaneously.

We got to my apartment and he told the guards to guard me. I was smiling on my way to my unit while being escorted by the guards. It was a horrible night, but Aaron made me feel better again with his chivalry. I couldn't believe how I felt, so much that I started getting more frustrated that I was stuck in a nightmarish marriage. I just knew from how Aaron treated me that there are men who would appreciate me and who would treat me better than Adam ever can. The agonizing memory of living as Adam's wife for the three years, being abused and brainwashed about men and the dark conditions of the world, brought more resentment to how I felt for him.

21

MASTER'S NEWBORN

It was safe for me to stay at the apartment for another month. Adam had to stay at his mom's for the month to take care of her house, while she was gone for the holiday. I was able to feel safe at home when Aaron dropped me off. For the next few days, I spent a lot of time walking around the unit, talking to friends and family on the phone, all day and night. I opened up to more people this time, unable to have any rest other than when I passed out.

The first person I contacted was Dee, who eventually moved to Bali. She was the best person to understand how I felt about all the odd mentalities I experienced. We talked on a messenger app.

Dee: Does he say God tells him to beat you? *rolls eyes* Crazy fanatics.

Me: He was actually saying that he can do that to me.

Dee: Oh God, I feel so sorry babe. No he can't.

Me: It's okay.

Dee: Islam says you can't just beat your wife.

Me: Yeah I had to fight with him about that for the longest time, it was so traumatizing.

Dee: Why does he beat you?

Me: A lot of random things. He can't control his rage. Like one time he beat me while screaming out that I don't like his mom. But you know what? I never said a single thing like that at all. So I got suspicious since then and wondered if his mom lied to him about something. And since then I started noticing how his mom hates my guts in every way possible.

Dee: Oh my God. You mean when we were hanging out, he was already beating you?

Me: Yes, when we would hang out and all, it already happened before.

Dee: Oh wow I had no idea. What does he use to beat you? Does he ever say sorry?

Me: His bare hands. He doesn't say anything. He so-called 'pinched' me last night repeatedly (he was actually grabbing me with his nails and as if I was a cat to carry out from the drain) and I ended up with torn skin and dark purple bruise covering my upper arm. When I cried, he said he would pinch me anyway. But obviously that's not a normal pinch at all. I have a huge blood clot and tears on my arm from that.

Dee: I hate Malay men more and more now. Bloody hypocrites. How do you keep it inside all this while?

Me: I'm literally waiting for justice from God.

Dee: To be honest, I felt like you were a prisoner in that awful house. Like you could never go anywhere or do anything.

Me: I think I'd rather be single, LOL.

Dee: Yes. And free. You graduated, right? You could apply for jobs outside, like Singapore or Australia.

Me: Still thinking of what to do but mostly gonna focus on making my next move light. Gonna try and reduce all my belongings, etc.

Dee: Well where would you like to go? Do you know that Australia has a working holiday visa option for people under 30? Why don't you apply for that?

Me: Okay, yeah I checked it out and I want that. I'll be planning my trip there then. Thank you. :)

After looking into the visa for Australia, I organized whatever I needed to prepare. Then, I wanted to know what Aaron would think about me leaving town, so I met him when he was going for supper. Adam was still never around at the time. He was still at his mom's for the month. I sat across Aaron while he had fast food.

"How did your mom go through her divorce?" I asked him.

"She got it bad," he told me. "My dad screwed her over and now she owes him millions," he said.

"What? Millions?" I asked him. I was shocked and I imagined myself being screwed over, too. No way I was going through court and risking that. "How does she deal with that?"

"She says she's waiting for justice from God," he told me.

I gasped. "That's like me, too! I say that. When people wonder how I go through it, I tell them I'm waiting for justice from God," I said, feeling happy with the similarity.

He watched me.

"By the way, I'm running away to Australia," I told him.

"That's not a good idea," he said so quickly, so confident, and serious.

I immediately wanted to laugh and giggle. I thought it was so cute.

"Why?" I asked, holding it all in with a smile.

"Well, what are you gonna do there? Do you know anyone there? Will you have a job?" he asked me so seriously.

I was still amused, but I got serious about it, too.

"I only know two people there so far, and maybe I can find more people if I get my social media up again," I answered. I couldn't stop wanting to smile. "And anyway, I don't care," I said with a shrug. "I just wanna go," I said.

On the way back home, Aaron and I had a quick heated debate on what I should do. He suggested that I use the law. I got quiet. I was quite aroused by how he was able to debate with me without rage. He was passionate, but there was no rage. He wasn't banging on his steering wheel, or banging his head on it, either. I almost forgot what that was like. It felt so fresh, like I was in a new world. I felt my heart beating fast. I felt resentment, thinking of how Adam disrespected me so much while I honored him as my husband. I also knew Aaron was right, but the law still seemed so impossible to me.

I gasped, and said, "I know…! How about I kill him?"

"Well, first of all, don't tell anyone!" he answered me, while looking at me to see if I was serious or if I was joking. I could tell he thought I was joking.

I burst out laughing to myself. It was too funny. Of course I needed everyone's opinion.

"Yeah, you know that switch that people get and then they just kill someone? I know that now! Now I understand murderers! I can't believe it!" I said to him, so merrily.

I could tell I was actually freaking him out. It didn't matter if I really understood murderers or not. I still didn't mind Adam being dead to pay back all that he's done to me.

Aaron was distracted in his thoughts, using his phone that was on the windshield, while driving.

"I knew you'd be open to talk about this. You're like my brother, you know, he would be cool to talk about this," I told him. No, actually, I never even tried talking about it to my brother.

"Yeah!" he agreed while I was talking. "Your brother…" he said after, while still using his phone and driving at the same time.

"Yeah, my brother," I said. "He's cool, you know, like you."

We reached my place at the same time.

"Anyway, hope you don't feel uncomfortable about anything. You know, I don't really feel like I'm married," I told him.

"Yeah, and you know about me and my girlfriend," he said to me. He reminded me of his relationship that was going dead.

I got out of his truck and left. I don't even think I said bye to him.

I think I was so anxious that I just didn't know where to go with the conversation. I never thought twice about anything. But I'm glad that happened. It got me to realize the extent of damage Adam had done to me. I wanted to get rid of him even more. It was slow burning, but I had the rage in me, getting ready for the ultimate boil.

I met Nate the next day for a lunch meeting at a cafe. He was big for a Malaysian. I met him like nothing happened between the years of not seeing him. His calm and serious aura that says 'I don't accept bullshit' made him the perfect civil lawyer to help me. Which he has, like Tina, for the past few years of my marriage when I would contact them.

Nate and I sat outside. He sat across me, relaxed with his back leaned on his seat.

"Are there biased and corrupt people at the court?" I asked him, worried that Adam would use his Malay speaking charms on any typical Malays, against me.

I didn't understand what Nate was answering me. It sounded like he was making excuses for their corruption, or that the corruption wouldn't be able to happen, or something.

The busy road next to us was loud with the sounds of cars, too.

I didn't really care about it anymore.

As standard procedure, I asked him, "What if I kill him?"

Nate was so serious about it. He answered with all the things to be aware of and cautious about, and all the things that can happen. If I were to get caught, for example.

He was scaring me with his seriousness. I felt like I was really going to.

Then he also said, "If you kill him, people will suspect that you want his insurance money."

So I got reminded of Adam's money that was less than mine, and the insurance that he didn't even have. However, I had insurance, during the times Adam almost killed me. It made me wonder if he had my insurance in mind. Would be a worse heartbreak if he did, if he was using me for personal gains. He even knew I added his name in my will. Then I stopped paying for my insurance after the first two years, because I was still not getting proper income, and I had to slow it down big time with all that I was spending on with my savings every month.

Moreover, wanting Adam dead for his money would have been a joke. I was never attracted to money or material things, especially not when it comes to love. I had rich men with just one of their cars worth more than everything Adam has ever owned, wanting to take me out, but I chose Adam because he wanted to marry me straight away, and especially because I thought he had relatively high morals. I thought he passionately loved me. I was fascinated. And maybe he did love me with passion, but he was perspicuously nuts about it. We were financially stable, but Adam was relatively poor compared to many of the other eligible bachelors. Certainly, money's good to have, but it can't possibly buy me love.

I didn't tell Nate that, though. He was so serious, in fact, he successfully ended all the cynical fun I was having. I didn't even get to laugh at all. Nothing was funny. After my meeting with him, I read about women in prison. More than half of them killed their husbands somehow. I even watched some YouTube shows of them. I imagined myself being so fucked in prison, figuratively and literally. I'd probably be a toy for them.

I met Tasha after that. She was one of my closest friends that I've known since my high school days. We still met up once in awhile throughout the years, and we never lost touch. She got married, had a baby, and got divorced. I went through it with her, emotionally. Her husband was a local Malay man and he was abusive, too. He sent lying messages to her mom, and had similar attitudes towards things, as well. Now is that even a coincidence? Or is it once again, the typical Malay mentality? She made about eight police reports, and went to the Syariah court twice, only to get rejected every time. They finally accepted, only after he hurt her baby. How screwed up was that? They made the baby get hurt first. And they think this is what God wanted for women, after all the lessons of honoring women? How sickening. This is what I meant about getting the divorce myself throughout the years. I knew from Tasha's experience that it wasn't going to be easy.

I believe in God's words, but not at all what men have interpreted and manipulated it to be. How can we say an unequal treatment, specifically the lack of support for one gender over the other, is the correct way? I completely understand why some people would rather not say that they're Muslims at all in this day, even if they find it to be a beautiful faith. They would only be seen as biased and uncivilized, because what else other than 'biased' and 'uncivilized' should we call such judicial system?

Tasha and I walked around a mall with her toddler, who was busy playing around us at the bookstore. We sat at the kids' section on the little chairs and talked quietly. No one was around, other than some people popping their heads in our view once in awhile.

"What if I kill him?" I asked her.

"Well don't tell anyone!" she said.

I laughed. I had clear flashbacks of when I thought I was going to die. It filled me with vengeance. I felt like it was my right to justice so much that I didn't even feel scared.

"No, don't kill him. I'll kill him," she said.

I laughed again. She was putting me in a lighter mood.

I answered with a laugh, "No, don't kill him. No one should kill him. Only I should."

Then Tasha told me about how I could disappear and the marriage would be annulled, or something like that.

"You're welcome to stay at mine for as long as you want. You can stay with me till you figure out what you wanna do," she told me.

"That's awesome, thank you so much… so I'll disappear to yours for a few months, and then I'm free," I repeated it.

"Yeah," she confirmed it.

"Okay, I really need it to work," I told her.

"Don't worry. I really wanna help you because I know what it's like," she said.

It gave me hope. I got excited to just disappear for a few months and start fresh.

Once I was done sharing with others who I felt would be able to help me, too, I picked Adam up at his mom's. He wanted to sleep at the apartment for the night. I brought up the divorce again, kindly, when we got home. But he ran out without warning. I contacted him on the phone via a messenger app:

Me: I need you to understand why I can't go on. Talk to me and work it out if you want me to stay. If not, then I can't. It's been too much already. I owe this to myself. And you owe this to yourself too. Be happy that we got to experience what it's like while we're still young. Honesty would be best for everything.

Adam: I have already been honest.

Me: So be honest about this. I'm not your slave.

Adam: Everything I said before. You don't listen to me. You don't want to listen to me.

Me: Listen to what? Listen to what you want me to be? A slave?

Adam: I'm just a dirt bag peasant that resells drugs. I don't even stop you from going out. And yet you wanna say all this crap.

Me: You stopped me a lot of times before. I couldn't see anyone. Even your mom did that.

Adam: Are we still at her's? Did you not go out just now?

Me: We wasted 2 years. You thought it was good to be a leader like that. Nothing worked. You beating me to speak Malay, to cover up, to like your mom out of nowhere, etc. None of that worked, they all gave the opposite effect.

Adam: We are at our own place.

Me: It's been bad here too. For a year you had no excitement
about the place at all and never want anyone to come over.

We continued talking in circles, not moving anywhere in the
conversation. I never called him a 'dirt bag peasant that resells drugs',
by the way. Not even anything close to that. I was just used to him
insulting himself, as if they were tools for sympathy, or just plain
trolling sarcasm. I started talking about the two divorce options
we could go through. There was a mutual one called 'Fast Track',
which can be finalized anytime within six hours, and the other one
is to go through at least three months of the case in court, meaning
we would be fighting against each other, with our Syariah lawyers.
However, if we were to choose the latter, Adam would undoubtedly
be in very big trouble. When I was done explaining the different
options we had, of course, as usual, he randomly changed the topic
entirely, distracting the problem by emotionally manipulating me for
sympathy. I was so angry.

Adam: Why don't I spend that money and get you a spa massage
and cupping?

Me: Spend what money...?

Adam: Whatever I have left after paying the rent

Me: I'm talking about divorce because you abuse me in many ways
and call me your slave. I never said anything else.

Adam: You're not my slave

Me: That's not what you said and it's gonna take a lot more than
just 'you're not my slave' to convince me. None of the abuse
says otherwise. I almost died so many times.

Adam: You're not my slave. You already went out without telling
me where you are and I didn't get angry. You just wanna

suddenly bring up the past again after picking me up. I tell you how I feel and you don't listen at all or say anything.

Me: Of course you can't get angry now. You know I already asked for divorce and I can be gone anytime. Of course you gotta shut up to keep me somehow.

Adam: Yeah that's all you talk about. You don't actually talk to me about something, only about how I control.

Me: What is this 'something' to talk about exactly when you want to control everything? Any idea?

Adam: You don't even talk about a problem like I'm an equal, and you talk about control.

Me: You called me a slave and now suddenly I'm also accused of not talking like you're an equal? Seriously? Is that all you got?

Adam: Stop bringing up the past.

Me: Too bad that's how divorce is. Keep up with the program.

Adam: You can say anything you like when you're angry.

Me: And you don't get to? Is that what you're saying?

Adam: You do as you want, you don't have to tell me where you go.

Me: I had little to no freedom to go out as I wish without getting bothered about it. Just because I have this past week doesn't mean anything. You sulk every time and you complain every time still, but you're dealing with it just because you know you screwed up like no other.

Adam: If I'm sad, you don't have to make fun of me sulking. I don't say anything in the end. I don't even mention it when I see you again.

Me: If you're sulking all the time then how is it that you're fine with me having freedom?

Adam: Who was sulking today?

Me: Sulking so much to the point of Wema (Adam's Arab friend who was always nice and friendly) messaging me about how you're stressed. Pleaaaase. Does he know how I've been??

Adam: He didn't even see me today. And I told him nothing is wrong.

Me: It doesn't change the fact that when I go out once in a blue moon, you still have to be a sulking child about it all day and night. And it doesn't change how superior you've been thinking you are all this while, fantasizing being my master and abusing me, calling me your slave, treating me like an object, not listening to my feelings at all ever, not comforting me at all ever as well, and it's even worse that I don't even have the luxury to exaggerate about it. So please quit the crap. Get real.

Adam had no answer. At first, all I thought was that it was so frustrating beyond belief to get some sense into him. I didn't realize how hopeless his condition really was, until Nate pointed it out to me. Adam still tried to use distraction, and he obviously knew I was right, but he still showed no remorse at all for anything he had done to me. I knew he was using emotional manipulation a lot, trying to make me feel bad. But it only just occurred to me of what that really meant. It really just meant he didn't care about abusing me at all. In fact, it was that way throughout the entire three years. Not even once did he feel sorry for his actions. He only ever cried like an expert, in order to win me back. But he never really cared about what he did at all.

I had never cried as much as I did throughout the entire marriage after that realization, thanks to Nate. I spent day and night crying. I woke up, and I cried. Before sleeping, I cried. In between calls and messages, I cried. It was almost like I was mourning his death. The death of a man I thought I knew. The death of a man I thought Adam was. I was alone anyway, so it really did feel like he was dead.

After a few days of mourning for Adam, I met Tasha again. I brought some of my clothes to hers for me to run away there.

We sat on her bed with her toddler. She was entertaining herself, watching videos on Tasha's phone.

"They will label you as 'janda', and look down on you," Tasha said.

"Oh, okay," I answered, and looked at her baby, not really taking it seriously. Even though I didn't know what that meant.

"No, it's an insult. They call you 'janda' as an insult," she made it clear to me.

"What?" I was shocked. I looked at her, trying to see if she was joking.

"Yeah. They don't treat divorced women the same. They'll really look down on you," she said. She was very serious.

"That's so messed up…" I said.

I got worried. I was so sure to leave Adam, but I didn't want to be labelled. How was that fair at all? Just because I got married to an abusive man, I had to be insulted for the rest of my life? What a screwed up, uncivilized mentality these typical Malays have.

After my meet with Tasha, I continued feeling depressed while doing research on Australia, to prepare myself for my new life. I was sure I didn't want to be in Malaysia after I get the divorce. Towards the end of the week of crying, I couldn't accept any of it anymore. I was on the edge. I felt I had nothing to lose. I was an abused wife, and I was a slave to a pathetic man I was conned into marrying. I was about to be labelled as 'janda', and I was about to risk my savings that the man I trusted my life with, never even helped to secure.

I thought to myself, if I'm his slave, then why don't I treat him how slaves would treat their evil masters? Abused slaves wish for their master's' death, don't they? They wish for someone to shoot their masters dead, then come into the shed where they're locked in for their next beating, and rescue them, right? No one would understand such hope in the modern age, other than the captives themselves. No one would understand my need for this justice.

I didn't even see it as revenge. I felt that wanting him dead was just a plain, reasonable idea. Why should he reproduce? Why should he raise a family? Why should he have any rights anymore? Why should anyone like that live at all? He's only going to ruin the world. He's only making it worse for women.

I questioned myself a lot, and I spent time analyzing myself, and analyzing all that I did wrong to him, only to be here again. I still wanted him dead. I knew I was never perfect. I could have been a better wife in a lot of ways. But did I really deserve all the oppression, all the hushes, and all the beatings for however wrong I was, from the very beginning of the marriage? What did I do to deserve all that? Why should I be fine with his existence?

I wasn't crying anymore. I was done with sadness. I was lying down on the sofa, staring into space. I received a tempting idea from the devil himself. Figuratively, of course. The devil cared more about me than Adam. I took my phone that was waiting for me on the sofa back, to my right. I scrolled through my contacts list and I found the man I needed to end it all, once and for all.

I knew him for many years before I got married. I started avoiding him when he suddenly waited outside my house all day for me, then later rejected that it was considered stalking. He wasn't the first to do that. He's a Satanist. Mischievous, and just plain trouble. I asked to meet him again.

It was the darkest time I've ever been in. Not even the total of all the depressive years from my father's death could be as dark as the moment I met him. I can't say where he's from, but he was experienced in unusual crimes. You know, the kinds that would mysteriously be out in the news sometimes. He had options for how Adam would be dealt with.

We sat side by side under a dim yellow light, at his place.

He explained how the different options would work and what I had to do with the choices.

I couldn't hear a thing he was telling me after that. I stared into space in front of us, thinking about how my life was screwed up all these years and it would only continue being screwed up.

"I need him dead," I said.

I woke up from what felt like a trance. I looked at him. I was a little bit shocked. I couldn't talk even if I wanted to.

He immediately paused. He became more serious. He knew I was serious. He probably knew I've gone mental there. He probably didn't care, either. He took a last satisfying hit from his cigarette and threw the butt behind me. He blew out the smoke.

"I tell you what. You go home, have some rest, and take your time... then come and meet me when you're ready," he said.

He ushered me to my car as I followed along.

"I'm only doing this because there are two things I'm protective of. Women, and animals," he said. I believed him. I never saw him caring much about other men at all. He's not even the type to have a best friend. He would only have girls and cats at home.

I drove back home that night, paranoid on the streets. Every car that passed me was a hitman. They all became suspects. I was paranoid all the way till I got home, and I locked the apartment door. I felt so thankful that I made it home safely.

I checked every room and every window discreetly. I lied down quietly on the floor, on a Japanese tatami mat I got for the living room. I kept low, to be further away from any sniper's view. I didn't know what was happening to me. Why was I acting like I was the one to be killed?

I realized then that it was my guilty conscience acting up. I was almost unconscious, with my guilt completely taken over me. Oddly enough, even after acknowledging that it was guilt, I was still uncomfortable. I was uneasy for a few days, gradually decreasing, but the feeling was always there.

Throughout my guilt, I made myself think about why I wanted Adam dead. I mean, *really* think.

Adam oppressed me for three years, almost killed me many times, and was then about to make me go through a stupid label for divorced women, by stupid people, for the rest of my life, but why did I *really* want him dead? I snickered to myself. *As if* I needed any other reason. I definitely had valid reasons to want him dead. I was so sure of that. But the point is, actually, forgiveness. Why couldn't I forgive him? Why couldn't I spare him his life?

It was my choice again, to forgive. It would be my final mercy. So I chose to let Adam go. I hoped God will reward me for it one day.

I saw Mr. Hitman again for the update.

"I changed my mind. I can't do it," I told him.

We spent the rest of our time by his pool, in the dark, talking about people, and about life. I talked about Australia a lot, too. I was still excited to go there. So excited and optimistic when I imagined it, that I felt no pain from what happened with Adam.

But I was still distressed with the marriage.

I went home, and for a few days, I continued to convince Adam to divorce me. He finally agreed to the mutual 'Fast Track'. I promised him that I wouldn't even get half of all his money, if we went through the mutual divorce. The week after, we went together in the same car. Before we headed there, I had to stop by the bank to withdraw some money. When I got back in the car, Adam seemed anxious. He changed his mind.

"Get it done yourself," he randomly said to me. He ran off, leaving me in the passenger seat.

I didn't understand what happened.

I called him to ask where he went, and he asked, "Why do you care?"

It seemed as though he wanted to trick me with the emotions, again. If not, he wouldn't even answer the call. I've been abandoned by him too many times to know that this wasn't real. He was just trying to stall the divorce, as usual. I wasn't going to accept that. I already waited since the last week, because he promised this.

I got anxious with what Adam was trying to do, and I immediately messaged Tina about what happened. She called me straight away and told me to contact two Syariah lawyers she gave me numbers of.

Someone was honking behind me to drive forward when I was on the phone. So much was happening at the same time. I drove forward then I immediately scheduled a meeting with the two Syariah lawyers.

At the same time, Mr. Hitman asked to meet me at a cafe. I went to him as soon as I could, and sat across him at the cafe.

"You should go to Sisters in Islam, they're an organization that helps women," he told me. "Look it up."

I was so touched. He wasn't even Muslim. I looked it up on my phone and found that it was quite close to the cafe. Because I was in the area anyway, I got side-tracked instantaneously since then and I could only think of going there and getting it over with. I left him shortly after to visit them.

I finally got myself some real, grounded, unbiased help. I was ready for it. Sisters in Islam guided me through what I had to do, and what I had to be aware of through the typical expectations women receive.

Two days later, it was February 14, 2017. Valentine's Day.

Adam came to see me at the apartment. He was being very sweet to me, like nothing bad ever happened. I spent time with him like nothing was going on with me. But I knew it was just the same cycle all over again.

My first scheduled meeting with one of the Syariah lawyers was supposed to be on that day.

I didn't think Adam and I would be spending time together just because it was Valentine's. He never believed in celebrating anything or enjoying any special occasions at all, other than Islamic ones, because they would be against real Islam, according to him and his mother. He specifically told me we can't celebrate birthdays, either. He was so against it every time. Then occasionally had to make excuses for his mom changing her mind and asking for birthday gifts for herself every year, and also for wanting to celebrate Adam's birthday with her family. They both just acted dumb about it. If I ever questioned it, I was treated like I was difficult.

On the surprising Valentine's, Adam took me out for a sweet breakfast and bought me some kiwi and strawberries that were in a heart shaped container. It puzzled me. We weren't even normal at all for weeks. Maybe he was willing to treat me well on a special occasion, because of my persistence in getting the divorce.

I didn't know how to get out of spending the day with him without looking suspicious. I still had to play along, even in the bedroom. I wanted to cry, though, watching him spend time with me. I couldn't believe I was having romantic moments with someone I was so sure I couldn't trust at all anymore. I was scared. It felt dark and unpleasant. I had to completely cancel with the first Syariah lawyer. It was the only day he could meet me.

Two days later, on the day that Adam's mom was back from holiday, and Adam was supposed to be back at the apartment again, I decided to run away. I was exhausted, and I knew it was over for good for me. It didn't matter when I chose to end it, because it was still going to be sad anyway. After abuse, or after romance, it was still broken as shit.

I ran to my mom's with a small luggage bag of clothes. She wasn't all that surprised I was there, but she wasn't sure if it was truly over. After breakfast the next day, I assured her that it's really over for good, and we recalled what happened three years before, the time I wanted to marry Adam.

"I knew he wasn't good for you," my mom said. "I already told you... He has no proper job, no stable income, he's dependent on his mom... and he can't even make his own decisions."

"He had different businesses and he said he could," I said, feeling upset that I ever believed him.

"Yes, of course he's going to say that, because he wanted to marry you. Don't believe that stuff. He's not stable, and he's still so financially dependent on his mom," she said. "And don't believe all these people acting so religious. If you're really religious then you never have to show off to people, and imposing all the time. Your faith is in your heart, not in how you look or how much you talk about religion."

"Yeah, I didn't know they would be the opposite," I said, feeling fooled.

"And I'm so surprised that out of all the guys you knew before, you chose him... You know so many people! You had so many guys wanting to be with you. I'm surprised. You were always so social... You knew a lot of really attractive guys, too. They were so much better than him, and so much more successful, and mature."

I let out a big sigh for all my naiveness, and I said, "I know..."

It's so true. I felt so sad and stupid for ever being so gullible.

"I never trust all these people who show off how religious they are," she said.

"And now neither do I..." I answered quietly to myself.

22

MISSION IMPOSSIBLE

It was after my first meeting with the Syariah lawyer that I finally got to meet. It was the following weekend. Sunday, 8:20PM. I went in the cafe to meet Adam's cousin, Zaffri, who agreed to the meeting at 8:30PM. I was expecting my two civil lawyers, Nate and Tina, too, who agreed to help accompany me and make sure everything's okay. Just as my Syariah lawyer asked for me to do.

It was a corner cafe. There were two separate glass door entrances on two different walls with big glass windows surrounding each. Soft toned yellow lights, metal interior, with seats and tables of white painted wood and natural wood. A group of people using their laptops in one corner, some others on their own in the other two corners. I found a table in the last one, next to the cashier counter. So it wasn't really a corner, it was quite in the middle of the cafe.

Fifteen minutes later, Nate walks in casually with a plain, loose casual t-shirt. He looked around the cafe where there was nothing interesting happening, and he came to join me at the table to wait for Tina. Ten minutes later, Tina, tall and curvy, walks in with her thick, wavy long hair, and a smile. She was wearing jeans and a soft sleeveless top.

Nate and Tina moved to two tables across me. They seemed like they were having a nice time together, so I didn't bother them the entire time. I ordered a warm cookie that was too dry with excessive chocolate, then self-served a small glass of water. I occupied myself on my laptop.

About an hour later, Zaffri finally got there. Thin and tall, he walked in with a black t-shirt that says 'Sabr' in Arabic letters, which means 'patience' in English. Adam liked to wear the same t-shirt too, when he's late. Zaffri had his head bent down as if trying not to be seen by anyone the moment he entered, watching the floor to guide him quickly to where I was, on a mission.

We greeted each other as he sat down. I told him about us being under my three lawyers' supervision, including my Syariah lawyer, and I made it clear that I was getting the divorce, regardless of anything.

"My dad's a Syariah lawyer. He said that if you wanted to get the divorce, you would have gotten it," he said.

"Yeah, this is what I'm doing. This is why we're meeting," I said.

"You wouldn't be meeting with me if you really wanted the divorce," he said.

"Huh? God willing, I'm getting the divorce," I said. "God willing," I repeated myself slowly with my eyes wide.

"Yeah, you would already get the divorce if you really wanted it, instead of offering all these options," he said.

"Why don't you understand kindness? Why don't you understand that some people desire more rewards from God for being kind?" I asked. It was, after all, my choice. I could have told my Syariah lawyer more about Adam and Khatijah, but I chose not to.

Zaffri was quiet. He had nothing to say.

With the list of things to tell him that was on my laptop, I spent a while explaining to him about the two different options of divorce for him to kindly tell Adam, which was the whole point of the meeting. But he suddenly started focusing on the money part.

"No, you can only get allowance during 'iddah' (waiting period after divorce when the woman can't marry another man and can't really go out of the house unless it's necessary), which is only --"

"No, I didn't say --"

"Don't interrupt me," he said sternly. He was blinking his eyes with a slightly tilted head and pointed finger at me, warning me not to correct him. "It's very rude. This is what I tell Azila (his wife), too. She interrupts me when I'm talking and I tell her it's very rude," he defensively said, as if casual conversations are supposed to be robotic and formal, with no corrections allowed to save time.

I didn't agree with him, but I've had worse from Adam with his hushes.

Zaffri continued, "You can only get money from Adam during 'iddah', and only if it's within his means, and only if he can afford it."

"No, wrong. That's not the only thing I can get," I said, thinking how odd he was to always shamelessly fight for things he didn't understand, but I should've known.

They had a quiz game in the family group chat for a family day once, towards the end of my first year of marriage. Even though I joined in later and Zaffri was playing from the beginning, I was suddenly winning. They changed the game a lot of times, and I was still winning. I thought it was all fine until Zaffri's mom, Aunty Lang, started being rude to me about it, practically bullying me openly in the group chat, implying how impatient I was. Her only reason was that I was winning, as she asked me later on, "Why can't you just let other people win?" I was appalled by her behavior, so I answered back, making it clear to her how ironic she was being, about patience. Zaffri who was almost a decade older than me, suddenly followed his mother and started attacking me with irrational insults that have no substance, too. I didn't need all that. Why couldn't they just save me the trouble and say, 'No one is actually allowed to win the game, unless you are blood related to us and your name is Zaffri'? Soon after, the possibility of Aunty Lang having symptoms of dementia occurred to me. She's not a stupid mean person! I thought. I told them about it, sharing them links for awareness and more info, just in case. It should be talked about casually. After all, Malays commonly call themselves 'nyanyuk' in their daily lives, which means dementia. I could've sworn I heard Aunty Lang call herself 'nyanyuk' before, too. But of course, Zaffri continued on with the irrational insults again, practically crying clueless through the insults, accusing me of diagnosing his mother this time. 'Dementia', he said, means 'autism'. He said it to me so snappy in the group chat. I've had years of practical and theoretical knowledge of psychology, old folks, and special children, since I was a teenager in Texas. I tried correcting him, but he was very aggressively persistent with it and wouldn't accept it. It was too ridiculous. Khatijah enjoyed the drama so much that she kept pressuring Adam about it, to the point of him contacting my mom to tell her I started problems. My mom just ended up being blessed to know that my in-laws were just unpleasant and jealous, without me even having to talk about them. That was the last time I chatted with them, ever.

"My dad's a Syariah lawyer," Zaffri said, defending his argument, as if it was supposed to make me see him as a Syariah lawyer too.

"Nope. That's not what my Syariah lawyer said," I shook my head.

"My dad's a Syariah a lawyer," he repeated himself like I didn't hear him the first time, nodding his head slightly as if saying 'Did you know that', waiting for a reaction from me like I was supposed to say, 'Oh my I didn't know! From now on you're right about everything, son of a Syariah lawyer!'. Zaffri continued, "You can't just get however much you want --"

"That's not what I said," I pointed to the list on my laptop to make him understand better, and started talking more sternly. "It says, 'divorce period'... Not, 'iddah' period... They're two different things. 'Iddah', is after divorce."

He paused. "Well, are you divorced?" he asked.

"No...? Isn't that the whole point of why we're here...?" I said, feeling like I was wasting my IQ in the conversation and debates of nothing. "Anyway, I don't even care about the money, that's like nothing. I just want out. Did Adam tell you anything about the abuse?"

"Uh," he answered. "Yeah," he nodded. Then he mumbled, "He said he hurt you, once, or twice, a little bit."

I almost laughed out loud. A little bit? Once or twice?

"He abused me once a month," I said.

"Once a month…" he repeated me in a low, distrusting tone.

"Yeah, once a month," I said, more clearly. "Here, look through the photos."

"Ooh…" he said slowly in a low tone, as he went through them, not knowing what to say. "I hurt Azila too, but not this bad."

"You hurt Azila?"

"Yeah, twice, but not like this," he said. He stopped going through the photos suddenly and asked me, "Why. Why would he do that?"

"I don't know? Because he's insecure?" I answered, not knowing why it was even important then.

"He's insecure… Why, why would he be insecure?"

"Um… I don't know, because some men are insecure with strong women," I shrugged with my eyebrows raised, vainly, knowing I was claiming myself to be strong.

"What did you do to him for him to abuse you?" he asked me.

"What? Are you saying that physically harming someone can be justified?" I asked him, only realizing that he was meaning to blame me.

He paused and looked away while starting to explain it while I interrupted him again.

"Are you saying that physically harming someone can be justified?" I asked, not believing that he really was justifying men abusing wives.

Then he started telling me a metaphorical story of a lion getting angry for being provoked.

I thought, well, Adam did grow out that big afro-type hair that one time and beat me like a caveman. His hair was long, thick and wavy, often messy, he looked completely possessed by a demon when he was angry and I had the most chills up my spine just looking at him. But what? This lion story is like saying you can't harm your wife unless you can no longer handle being a husband. A lion is a wild animal. When provoked, it's still a wild animal. Adam was my husband. When provoked, he should have still been my husband. And what does being a husband mean? Certainly not the right to abuse his woman like she's a punching bag! He couldn't even have the decency to divorce me first!

My face and eyes responded that it was an awkward moment. He was still insisting that I could have been responsible for the abuse I received throughout the years. As if I wanted to die, provoking Adam for all those years, for super fun near death experiences, for the awesome damages to my body in order to be physically disabled one day.

"I'm sorry you had to hear this from me," I said, "You don't know Adam and his mom. No one knows them. I've lived with them for years. I should know them best."

"You shouldn't be talking about them like that," he said and shook his head so righteously.

"Look, do you know the psychology of psychos? Do you know the psychology of abusive people?"

He shook his head in response to each and said, "No."

"Exactly," I said.

"It's normal, it's a culture thing," he said.

Bingo. The solid answer I've been searching for.

Zaffri continued, "You're not used to it because you have a different culture. Abuse is normal for us. A lot of us, many of us, witnessed Adam getting abused by his mom when he was growing up, too." He was looking down, eyes wide, as if seeing the scenes in front of him, and continued, "He was abused, a lot... And I was abused, too. But many, many of us have seen his mom abuse him, a lot. Azila doesn't understand it either, she grew up with an all loving culture... So it's just a culture thing. We just have different cultures."

Someone else in the family also once revealed to me that Adam was abandoned from care when he was young. His mom didn't even know what to do with him. I pitied him so much when I heard that in the first year of our marriage, I kept trying to help him with it. I was very protective of him even after getting abused by him. But then I realized that we all have gone through sufferings in the past, in our own ways. Of all suffered children, why does he get to be an asshole? It made me sick thinking about it. It was his choice to not overcome it, just as it was Khatijah's choice to not overcome her issues, too. No wonder Adam abused me, abandoned me, and hushed me so much. That's most likely all that he experienced from his mother. And they accept all this? I would have alarmingly called Child Protection in a heartbeat, as I have done before. Things like this shouldn't be taken lightly at all.

"Okay well, I needed you to talk to Adam for me because he's in an unreasonable state of mind," I said.

"Oh, now you're accusing Adam of having a mental illness," he said, shaking his head so righteously, again.

"I didn't say that? Don't put words in my mouth," I said.

Mental illness is an actual disorder. It can't be a state of mind. It's not a state of mind. Even if Adam really was mentally ill, it wasn't right for Zaffri to twist my words right then. But of course, Zaffri liked to mix words up, with just about anything that sounds similar to him. I wouldn't have mind any of his confusions when he talked to me, at all, if he didn't have such a bad attitude about them. I can be tolerant with ignorance a lot, from my own experience of not knowing a lot of things, too. But having a bad attitude about it is just too annoying. Everyone has their weaknesses. But fighting about what you don't understand is just so rude!

"Then why do you say he's in an 'unreasonable state of mind'?" he asked.

I just asked him, "Did you not see the evidence?"

He had no answer and his eyes were looking around, trying to think of something to say in defense. He looked away without an answer, slightly shaking his head, and sighed with annoyance.

"Your Syariah lawyers?" he asked, stiffly pointing behind him with his left thumb, as if he wasn't allowed to face them.

"They're two *civil* lawyers… Under the supervision of my *Syariah* lawyer…" I said to him slowly. My irritation was pretty obvious by then.

"Okay," he said silently and nodded slightly. Then in a split second he put on a serious face and started shaking slightly, and said, "Anyway, I don't think this is going anywhere. Oh and by the way, I've been recording the conversation." He pointed to his phone, while waiting for my reaction.

It was quite funny, as if that was all his mission was about all that while. That he had to walk in with his head down and everything, to avoid my lawyers he probably saw through the glass walls while waiting outside to observe, and then to record me the entire time. I obviously had photos of him to easily show my lawyers, too. What a task. I had a three-year mission I was about to end, and he seemed to be so proud to have a single conversation recorded.

I just looked at his phone, looked at his face, and looked at my phone.

I wasn't sure why he seemed to be expecting me to be worried, considering everything in the recording were in my favor, and especially with the evidence of their abusive cult. Moreover, what he did was unethical, disrespectful, and considered a form of abuse even by law. It was already evident that they have an abusive culture; that not only are they abusive by nature, but they were proud to be such a cult, too. They seemed to be just shamelessly sadistic, all the time. Regardless. It's their way to get respect, and they would even justify their incivilities rather than taking responsibility and feeling any remorse.

"Okay wait, let me message my lawyer," I said calmly, quickly picking up my phone to my left. He was shocked, watching me. I looked up and I asked him, "So what did your dad say again? Abuse is okay?"

His face started shaking, boiling.

"What?" I quickly asked, as if I didn't know what his problem was. "I'm talking to my Syariah lawyer!" I pointed to my phone.

He picked up his phone and started talking to the bottom speaker to record himself, "She's lying now, about my dad. And it's... 10:15PM, I'm leaving the cafe now..."

I was distracted while messaging my Syariah lawyer, but as he quickly grabbed his things and got up to leave, I managed to wave at him and say to him nicely, "Bye, Assalamualaikum!"

"No. You don't have to act like that," he scolded me, for wishing him peace in Arabic. "Now I know you," he said threateningly, impulsively bringing his tablet close to my face all of a sudden and held it there, then he stormed off.

How rude!

Nate and Tina made me feel better with all their law stuff, after. I was so disrespected throughout the entire conversation, from beginning to the end. There was no sense of responsibility. There was only attack.

My Syariah lawyer instantly answered me, saying, "Please remember that no abuses are justified. Don't worry, God will be with you. Remember, you met his cousin for an amicable resolution. If the other side refused to acknowledge that, it is not your loss, it is theirs. If that's what the other side is expecting, God willing that's what they will get. We will meet tomorrow for the next course of action."

23

THE END

When my mom heard about what Zaffri said and did to me, it really aggravated her. My mom has always been so patient with unreasonable people and always believing that the world is so beautiful with good people who have good intentions. It affected me so much throughout my life that it got me to believe the same about Adam and Khatijah, too. But what Zaffri said and did to me really woke her up. She was appalled by how nasty the family really was. Her boiling point was rising.

"The whole family's just going to justify what Adam did, too," I told her.

"Why would they do that?" she asked me. "Are they not educated?"

"I don't know," I shrugged. "That's what happened with his cousin. So why wouldn't the rest of them do the same? Maybe they're all more biased than educated," I told her.

"Why would they do that? They don't know what's right and wrong?" she asked me.

I shrugged again. "I don't know," I answered. "I can see them being like that. Just like how his mom has been lying about me to her friends. They can just use lies. Create a sad story for Adam. They have a different culture, anyway."

"I didn't know they were a cult? I've been so patient with them. If they're really justifying Adam's behavior, I'm going to tell everyone how they've really been," she said. "I don't care. I'll even go deep into their companies. I know where they work and I know the people there. I never thought they were like this… But if they really intend to ruin you like this, if they really want to ruin you, I'll just speak the truth about them to everyone. I never wanted to have to do this. I will, if they're really asking for it... And I'm going to contact my lawyers."

She went through her phone. My mom had her own lawyers, too. She knew them since maybe before I was born. I even knew one of the top lawyers in Malaysia, who people say is the real deal. I never wanted to have to contact him, though, because I would have to contact his son, who I stopped being in touch with all of a sudden. Having said that, he was always a great guy and we always clicked. Nonetheless, my case was supposed to be so simple. It's just a divorce. That's all I wanted. A divorce.

My mom even took time off her busy schedule to meet my Syariah lawyer. I was secretly happy. I was so glad Zaffri did what he did. I got to have more of my mom in my story.

My mom and I sat in the meeting room with my Syariah lawyer.

"She thinks that everyone's going to justify Adam's behavior," she told him. "But how can that be? How can educated people think like that?"

I gave a big shrug to him, because I honestly don't know how. I don't know how people can be like that. Maybe they're not actually educated, but only disguised as educated.

My Syariah lawyer had the divorce request all prepared for me from the night before. I was to file it under 'irreconcilable differences'. He explained everything there was, to expect, if Adam still wanted to reject my request. We were to choose the kindest option, to deal with Adam, every time. However, whatever happens after every rejection, would only be of disadvantage to him. He then guided us through what had to be done, and we met the Commissioner of Oath together. Because Adam was persistently making me get the divorce done myself, rather than the mutual one, it was only reasonable that I filed the police report, too.

Till now, I still don't understand why Adam's family would rather

Adam have a criminal record. It wouldn't be good for anything, other than being in a reality show for criminals. Maybe they wanted me to go through a harder time, but again, every step was only worse for them in the long run. I did agree to helping them as much as I could, but they could never seem to calculate that.

It was after dinner two days later. I got to the police headquarters with Tina, after laughing a lot in the car. Some security guard that helped us through a shortcut just said "I love you" to us. It's pretty common in Malaysia, but it tends to make me laugh every time. I was rolling in the car seat like it was the funniest thing ever, unable to hold it in.

Many officers were around the guarded compound of the headquarters. We walked in the station together that was in the middle. It was bright like 7 Eleven after a night out and you can see how thick people's makeup are. There were two male officers sitting on the sofas to our left. One policeman and one policewoman behind the desk.

"I'd like to make a police report regarding domestic abuse," I said to them, as we sat down in front of the policewoman attending to us.

She talked to Tina for a bit, wondering if she has seen her before. In the meantime, the policeman asked me what we were doing there.

The policewoman opened the first envelope of photos that I brought for them, and she immediately shook her head and said, "Tsk tsk tsk, you were really patient with him."

I looked at the photos she was holding, and saw that they weren't even from the worst days. They were the better days! I felt horrible, knowing that I continued staying with him after all that. But I know the question should never be why I stayed, but rather, why did he have to hurt me? He was my husband, and that's all I could see. Why should I even question myself?

"Do you have these saved digitally?" she asked.

"Yes," I said.

I passed her my thumbdrive from my bag. She tried to connect it, but it wouldn't work. We had to type it out ourselves from what I had already printed out. Tina and I took turns at first, but she helped me type the rest of it. I had to talk to the Sergeant, who called to talk to me on their phone. I was surprised and impressed, considering we haven't been there for long. Malaysia used to have bad reputation with their police service. Surprisingly, I've only had really good service from them so far, even when they came to help me at the house that day. She asked me a lot of questions and I answered them, trying my best not to cry. I got off the phone with her.

"Do you want us to take action?" the policewoman asked, with pleasure for honorable adventure. The Sergeant asked me the same thing on the phone.

"No, it's okay," I shook my head and looked down, imagining what would happen to Adam. My stomach tightened.

"If he does it again, we will have to take action," she said, making it clear that I won't have a choice the next time they hear about it.

"Okay," I acknowledged her.

"Do you have a photo for me to see how he looks like?"

"Yes," I said, going through my phone and found a happy photo of us, "Here. He's handsome."

She looked at the photo for a while and said, "Is he?"

I looked at the photo on my own and frowned. He was still my husband. Adam was never my type before, or never caught my attention when I saw him, particularly because he appeared to be Malay with a different culture than what I was used to. It wasn't anything racist, as I had some other Malay friends, too, but it was his aura. He had a very local Malaysian aura that I didn't even know what it was. Only today do I realize that it was a typical Malay aura all along. He was a typical Malay, in white skin. Malay men are fine to me, but I certainly never wanted that typical mentality I was always warned about. They could never understand me, just as I experienced.

"Do you think he's handsome?" she asked Tina, while packing up the evidence.

"Knowing how he is -- no," Tina answered with certainty, with no interest in looking, busy typing the last few sentences.

I was silent, thinking about him.

I definitely know better looking men. Better in everything else, too, in every way. But I was a fool, so rigid by how much he wanted me, so fooled by his so-called moral values.

The policewoman printed out a copy of the report for me and wrote some numbers on it.

"Here," she passed me the copy. She pointed to the number, and said, "Contact the Sergeant directly if anything happens again."

Tina and I left the headquarters, and went in her car.

"That was so embarrassing, I almost cried just now," I said to Tina as she was driving me back to my car.

"It was when you were talking about Nur Hidayah," she said, while focused on the road.

The article was published just the month before, in January, and it shocked the heck out of me when I first read it two days before Valentine's Day. Nur Hidayah, a woman who stayed with her husband, Muidin Maidin, for ten years. She had children with him, tolerated his abuse throughout the entire marriage, made many police reports, and never got a divorce, to the point of him killing her in the end anyway. I found a photo of him online. Crying, while cuffed and held by a cop walking with him. It reminded me of how Adam would cry like a toddler in a similar way. How genuine the crying face is, with so much emotions. It can almost make you feel like letting him go. Just let the kid go already. Adam would be very dramatic, and a lot of times even stomping his feet. That could've been us in the article. The dead wife and the cry baby.

"Oh yeah," I said, recalling it again. With my voice cracking immediately, I held back my tears, shaking, I said, "I feel- so- bad- for her-…"

I managed to hold it in again. I didn't want to freak Tina out. She has helped me enough.

I know Nur Hidayah was nothing like me, but I empathized her, so much. I thought about her intensely. I cried about her on the way back to my mom's. I was crying my eyes out, sobbing. I never knew how much I could feel for another. I never knew how easy it was for me to feel the pain of someone I never knew.

I submitted the divorce request to the Syariah Court, then I was given the option to either have them send it to Adam, or for me to pass it to Adam myself. Passing it myself would be a lot faster, and I wanted that. We still had to meet in court after, so it would still be a long wait, to me. Not to mention the 'iddah' waiting period I would have to observe after the divorce, for a duration of three menstrual periods, as the woman. I wasn't allowed to have fun socializing for that long, just in case Adam wanted me back and we were to have sex. Which would automatically make me his wife again. I contacted him through a messenger app.

Me: When will you be free to sign the divorce papers? I need them back right after to send to the court.

Adam: You would rather follow a man made law than to talk to me. You're a quitter. You always have been.

Me: No, actually, we are following God's law, under the court of God. I'm sorry for all your bitterness, but I can't blame myself for your misery. I witnessed your emotional instability since before marriage, but I was too naive to realize what it all meant. I don't know everything, but I understand a lot about you and about us now after the 3 years. I heard about the abuse you had to go through as a child. I sympathize it, but I'm not responsible for it. Abuse is never easy for anyone, even if you wish to project it as the abuser. Justifying it only hinders mental development and risking your own sanity. No one deserves to be abused. It is your right to have a kind mother, and it is my right to have a gentle man. I have been patient with you for 3 years, and that's enough for me. It's my

God given human right to leave anyone who abuses me. It doesn't make me a quitter. It makes me a survivor. The court has already accepted the request and allowed me to send it to you myself. If you reject it, they will send their own men to send the second one to you. If you reject the second one, they will send a warrant of arrest. You can choose to respond however you want, but God willing the divorce will still happen.

He had no answer.

It was really annoying how he kept talking like he was willing to work things out so much, but every time when it came down to it, he would never deliver. What 'talk' did he want, when every 'talk' would only lead to abuse? Asking for a divorce after abuse makes me a 'quitter', to him, whether a real belief or just for manipulation. Then why don't he experience me beating him with a baseball bat once in awhile and see if he can still be okay with me as his wife, right? I highly doubt he would be able to handle it. He couldn't even handle imaginary problems and he beat me for them. It's really sickening how some people can think so highly of themselves to the point of expecting appreciation after all the abuse. To the point of still not seeing anything wrong with them or anything wrong that they've done.

My perseverance as a wife was always about my forgiveness, not about him. But it seemed as though he really believed he was something great, that he was above me for being a man. That not only was he the leader of my home for being my husband, but he was my master. How vain of him to think I was always there because I needed him. No, I never needed him. I was living on my own for years, doing much better in terms of everything. From the first month of being married to him, I already knew he was the worst guy I had ever been with, needless to say. I was loyal and merciful to him because I was his wife, not because my gender was of lower status.

Being a woman does not make me lower than men. My kindness was never a weakness. It was my choice to give him. It was my gift.

I left the divorce papers at night at the apartment and left notes on them since he wasn't going to be free for me to explain them to him in person. I gave him a weekend to read and sign them. I went back to the apartment in the afternoon when he was just getting up from sleep. He didn't sign them yet.

"Can you sign them?" I asked him. I flipped through the page for him to sign and said, "Here... Don't worry about all the other spaces, the court will take care of that."

He sat up with no words, with his head down, and signed them.

I kept the papers in my bag and I went around the apartment collecting more things I could carry back to my car.

I heard Adam crying loudly.

He went to the guest bathroom.

I felt a little worried, so I went to him. He slammed the door, while crying louder.

I decided to leave because I wanted to keep the divorce secure, and I didn't want there to be a huge drama to deal with again. I was already so close to being free.

I called the court before heading there, and they told me I could keep the papers with me. I didn't know that. I just had to make it there and submit it at the court on the scheduled date, which was a week from then.

It was finally the end. March 13, 2017. Almost our third year anniversary, that was in ten more days. It was at nine in the morning.

Adam and I went in the Syariah courtroom together. I was waiting for him before I entered. I also called him to be sure he was awake. I couldn't believe we were finally there. The whole room was all wooden brown. There were many other couples waiting to get divorced, too. Men and women were separated. Men were on the first two rows of seating, and women were on the last two. Adam and I sat at the very end, further away from the others, as if we were still together. It was just an event we were attending. I was sitting directly behind him. Everyone was facing the judge's bench that was in between two witness stands. In front of the judge's bench were two speakers' podiums to talk to the judge, with a desk in between, and one at each side. In between our seating and the judge's bench were meeting tables for Syariah lawyers.

We had to wait for a while for the judge. When he came in, we all stood up out of respect. Then we had to wait for him to be ready, and going through our requests. The room was so quiet. We weren't allowed to talk or use our phones. I sensed everyone anxious, but keeping calm. Some, like me, relieved to be there.

The judge called out the first couple. One lawyer answered to represent them. I wasn't quite sure what the lawyer said, but I understood that the couple weren't going through it that day. They had cancelled it. I would never forget how I felt when I looked at the back of Adam's neck when that happened. How it stretched out to see more of what was happening. The sadness I felt when I saw his behavior. He seemed to be in hopes that there could be a way out of the divorce. I knew him too well. He would be crying for this to be stopped by now. I felt sad. I still cared about how he was feeling. I had a lump in my throat but I remained calm. I had to focus on myself. He had three years to be a loving husband. He had the choice. He had it, every time. Why couldn't he just get it right? Why couldn't he just calm down and be a gentleman? I did try to work it out, didn't I? Why does he have to look down on women? Why does he see kindness as weakness? And why couldn't he just stand up for himself, against what was truly wrong in his life? He was given too many chances.

The judge called out the second couple. It was us. We walked up to the two podiums. He was on the left, and I was on the right. The judge asked us a few questions.

"Did you receive this request?" he asked Adam, referring to the request I submitted.

"Yes, I did," Adam answered.

"Do you understand it?" he asked.

"Yes, I understand what was stated on it," Adam answered. He was speaking in Malay, with big words. I assumed that was what he said. I liked how he spoke. I was impressed. Too bad that's not what I need in a marriage, though.

"Have you consummated the marriage?" he asked Adam.

"No," Adam said.

"No?" the judge asked in surprise, looking at us both.

"I mean, yes. We have," Adam said.

The judge laughed. "Okay, I have to ask this, because it's part of the procedure. If not I wouldn't ask that," he said, making it clear that we understand.

We both nodded while slightly laughing.

"How long have you been married?" the judge continued asking.

"Three years," Adam answered.

He looked at me and asked, "Are you pure?"

I wasn't sure what he meant by that, so I was hesitant.

"Um… yes," I said.

"Are you pure today?" he asked me again.

"Oh, yes, I am," I answered, only realizing that what he meant was whether I was on my period or not. I wasn't on my period, which meant that I was 'pure'.

"Here, you didn't state that you want any of his money or his belongings. Here at the Court, we're not responsible to arrange that for you. You must say it, if you want it. Are you sure you don't want anything from him?"

"Yes," I said and nodded.

"You're absolutely sure you don't want any of his money or his belongings?" he looked at me observantly, with his face pulled forward.

Adam turned his head to look at me. I felt that he was nervous from it.

I nodded with a smile and said, "Yes, I'm sure."

"Okay," the judge took note of it and seemed like he was thinking about us. We seemed so odd.

The witness in front of Adam passed him a piece of a paper to read the oath of divorce from.

"You may make the oath now," the judge said to Adam.

He started reading it with a shaky voice, like he almost cried. I felt sad when that happened, and I felt the judge and witnesses feeling sad for him, too. Then he cleared his throat quickly to continue with pride.

It was intensely emotional. I felt so happy for my freedom, but yet I was feeling so sad. I felt sympathy, both for him, and for myself.

24

HEALING

It's May, 2017. Here I am now, writing this book, while currently observing 'iddah', the waiting period after divorce. It should be over in just a few more days, after my third complete menstrual period. I will then officially be free.

For the past three months, I haven't been, and I still am not allowed to leave the house at all for fun. Only for necessary things. If Adam and I had sex anytime within the three months, for whatever reason, I would have immediately been his wife again. Luckily, I had already run away to my mom's before the divorce, which meant that I was able to observe it at my mom's instead of at the apartment with Adam. I spent the first month of 'iddah' moving all my things back to my moms, and settling into hers. I still did in this last month, too, to get some things I forgot at the apartment. Adam seemed to be having fun with a lot of friends there.

It's been awhile since I lived with my mom. I was then able to have some peace of mind. However, my joints still cracked from Adam's beatings more than a year ago. I got anxious flutters, for no apparent reason. I recalled the pain I went through throughout the marriage. I recalled when my butt was so bruised that I couldn't even sit on it and I had to lie down on one side when I wanted to sleep. I couldn't even go to uni. I suddenly remembered things I had repressed, from forgiving him.

I tossed and turned every night with cold sweat from vivid nightmares. I had an emotional break down before sleeping. I didn't want to be depressed. I went through years to get over my father's death. I wasn't going through crying myself to sleep anymore. I tried to heal myself emotionally and psychologically, but it was difficult to. So much of me felt like it was ripped off of me without consent. I spent every day researching on how to heal and to find myself again.

I went online to find some of my best friends who were in Texas, and in London, to distract myself. I missed them so much, and they reminded me so much of my carefree past. They reminded me of the real me, the me that was not violated by a cult. One of my best friends, Lauren, and I, used to spend time writing long letters to each other. Since junior high, we wrote long letters to each other to talk about everything we possibly could, so that we wouldn't miss a single thing from when we weren't together. I did that with my other best friends, too, but Lauren and I continued to online when I moved to Malaysia.

When I talked to her again, we were still as close as ever, but then I realized with a heavy feeling in my heart of how much of me was gone from the lives of my friends. I realized that I would eventually have to talk about the three years to almost everyone I knew, and it would be almost impossible to. It wouldn't be fair for me to spend years talking about this. I deserved to move on, as I've been wanting to, since Adam's first strike.

I still only wish the best for Adam, at the end of the day. However, I also realized that although I was once married to him, he's just some guy that abused me anyway. It wouldn't matter if he was a stranger in an alley or someone I was married to, he was still an abuser and an oppressor. Any of his supporters, too, would just be on that same boat.

Why should I continue dealing with the pain alone for years more?

My voice is no longer oppressed. I'm able to be heard again. I'm also able to make a living however I want to, again. I never felt happier to be able to have freedom, to be able to do anything I wanted to without anyone stopping me.

No, I don't need a psychologist to talk to, to guide me to a better life or to ask me how I feel. I've been my own psychologist. I know what I want for a better life. And I know how I feel. I've analyzed myself enough. I've analyzed a whole cult enough, too. I've spent enough time replaying the memories of what I went through. They're still the same.

I knew I had to write about it. Only a book would bring me justice. Only a book would help me through my healing. And only a book can reclaim what was once lost. What was once taken away from me. My work, my voice, and my freedom.

I know I made a lot of mistakes, especially the mistake of marrying Adam to begin with. I chose to see beauty where it was only irrational to. I gave my trust where it wasn't appreciated. I tried rationalizing the disrespect. I stayed out of sympathy rather than love. I went through years of what I knew was unfair. I allowed myself to be persuaded. I gave access to betray my trust repeatedly. I gave too much benefit of the doubt. I stuck to what I believed was the principles of marriage. Loyalty to a spouse.

I'm not going to be harsh on myself. I wasn't upset to have found a troubled family. I believe there's a reason for everything. Maybe I was meant to finally fix Khatijah's unusual, so-called 'Sunnah' Islamic ways. Maybe for Adam to finally get his mom told off for treating him like a slave, or for their cult to learn some sense, or to finally get Adam out of the house, to experience independence. I do hope Khatijah would spend on therapy for him and for herself, too, if she really loved her son at all. I hope she takes some real responsibility for what she had done to him, too.

I was so excited about Islam so much that I was learning all the positive things about it. So much that I was blinded with the belief that every Muslim were pleasant people. Perhaps it was a gift for me from God, to finally learn everything I wanted to about Islam, to see the most beautiful things that it has, and the ugliest, too. Only He knew the passion I had, and only He could have guided me to all the answers. Maybe it was for me to appreciate life more, too, and to quit being so depressed about my dad being gone. I certainly appreciate my freedom, my independence, and my life, like never before, now. Even when I'm still only in my 'iddah' period. Maybe it was everything that was meant to be. It was all of the lessons combined for a more beautiful, bigger picture.

I believe in the power of patience and forgiveness. If I didn't forgive Adam all those times, I may have never found all that I found throughout the three years. If I had gotten the divorce any earlier, I may have never found out about their cult, either. I was blessed with more answers than I ever asked for, just from being patient. I might have ended the marriage, with years of questions that may have never been answered at all. I do believe that God has helped me through all the findings at the end of it all, and that he has been all this while. He has answered my prayers for clarity and refuge, too, by giving me the three years of nightmare in my path. The entire experience now appears to be a spiritual reward.

I've learned that sympathy needs limits, and that not everyone is as genuine as their cheap words. I understand now why some people can never seem to smile back. I used to feel bad for people who can't seem to be happy or light hearted. I had the urge to cheer them up or make them have a better life somehow. I was confused when women in headscarves couldn't smile back, when we're really supposed to be sisters in faith. But I'll still be light hearted, regardless. God willing, these people can never bring me down. If they choose to be grumpy and cruel to me, that's something they will have to deal with on their own. That's their own soul that needs to call out to God.

In many ways, I'm almost nothing like how I used to be, from every trauma Adam has ever given me. In all that sense, the experience has helped me a lot in being the woman that I am today. Adam was an abuser, a fantasized slave-master, and a so-called husband, for me. It was horrifying, and I've been damaged in many ways, but those years will be a lesson I'll hold on to. I don't think any marriage can easily be forgotten. Whether I like it or not. The memories will be there.

I was so happy a few days ago, when I went out to run errands. I already went for my graduation ceremony last month, and I was feeling so excited for the end of my 'iddah' period.

I was at a shoplot. A gorgeous, classy older woman suddenly started talking to me.

"Where were you from, shopping? What do you do?" she asked me.

"Oh!" I was surprised she talked to me. "No, I'm free now, I'm always free," I answered her cheerfully with a big smile. "I don't have anything to do."

"You're always free!" she was surprised. "Then you should really enjoy this age."

"Yeah, I know..." I agreed with her, and continued our conversation about her marriage.

She had no idea. No idea that I'm such a young girl that went through marriage, abuse, and divorce. Who would ever guess? I was too happy. And it wouldn't have been appropriate for me to talk about my sorrows, however much I would have liked for her to understand me better. However, I don't think anyone really can understand, if they don't know what happened to me.

I feel blessed, because I've never felt so at peace on my own as I do now. I refuse to believe Islam is the problem at all. It's the people that make it a bad experience. There's a reason the Holy Quran is poetic. It's not just words of wisdom, but it's a beautiful piece of art. Just like poetry, and every art work, it's how you perceive it, that matters in the end. When I started reading the Holy Quran, I thought it was so beautiful and realistic. It doesn't sugarcoat the true nature of our existence. It awakens my fears and my hopes of the future all at the same time. When I read it, I felt the beauty, so much that I believed anything that made me feel uneasy couldn't possibly be from the teachings of Islam.

I still stand by my views today. We're all humans, and we sin every day. But it's not for us to tolerate those who would violate us.

There are limits to how much people can hurt us, and there are also limits to how much we can revenge. Especially when the revenge is uncalled for. Without these limits, we are nothing but animals at constant war. The bad apples in the Muslim community could never change my view of what Islam means to me, personally. Others' religiosity can no longer fool me. I'm not afraid of them, and I'm not afraid of Islam.

I wrote this book at times, shaking in tears. I wrote it in the hopes to be healed. I don't believe stories like this are meant to be kept hidden. Just as how I found hope through other women's stories online, I believe more abused women should speak out, too. Let our stories help other women. Let our stories be a reminder for Muslim men to respect their wives when they ask for a divorce, too. Let this be a reminder that Muslim women aren't afraid to speak, even if hushed and beaten for years.

May this book be amongst the many reminders of the reality of the Muslim community. Of the evil sides, regardless of the headscarves and the beards, masking them. Let it be a reminder of the things to focus on, if Islam is truly appreciated. Islam, frankly, can never make it in a civilized society if Muslims continue to treat women as second class citizens. That was never what God or any of His Prophets ever taught us. Never, ever.

The words of the Holy Quran will forever live, there's no doubt about that. However, Islam in a civilized society, may or may not make it, if the words are being read selfishly. With the lack of consideration for each other, for every gender, for other humans in the world, and people of various backgrounds and experiences. Such judgmental mentality in the Muslim community is in our daily lives. It shouldn't be taboo. It's time for Muslims to meet real civilization. The civilization in our minds. In our mentality.

I couldn't bear thinking that such a cult accepted amongst some Malay Muslims in Malaysia, or even in other countries, could possibly continue for generations more, and maybe till the end of time. The more we lack the of awareness of it, the more it seems taboo to even openly discuss it, and to educate. I knew I couldn't, and I shouldn't, be quiet about my story. I had a strong feeling I wasn't placed to experience such a cult just to be tested and move on. I was placed in it because I had the responsibility to tell it. For all that, this is it. It's about time we speak about what's evil, conclusively, in order to improve our love. It's about time we truly care for each other. And finally, it's about time that we all heal.

AFTERWORD

"I fell for it. I believed him. I felt sympathy."
– Liya Red, Trust Overboard, Ch. 6

Liya Red's maiden book touches on the complexity of the experience of domestic abuse survivors summarized in that three simple lines. Simple but with profound impact on their lives. The book begins with the beginning of an end, and concludes with healing – a journey that takes us back in time to understand the struggles of living in an abusive relationship, peeling back every layer of emotions, and uncovering every shade of manipulation.

While there are many theories surrounding why and how abuse happens, it doesn't get as raw and emotional as reading a first person's recount of the incidences. Taken as individual events, peppered across a length of time, some conclude that they aren't a big deal. Liya, however, forces us to acknowledge that abuse is not only that which ends with physical violence, but those subtler forms of power and control dynamics that happens on a daily basis, too.

In many parts of the book, you would find yourself thinking, "this is it, she is gonna leave". The fact that she doesn't may upset you, but such is the reality of many survivors who try very much to save their relationship whilst facing frustrations and comments from relatives and friends around them. Trust Overboard explores the reasons why it is not easy for women to pick up and leave, and the trajectory that they go through before reaching the limits of their patience. Judgment is the last thing they need nor is helpful at this state, and this book could help us as readers to come to terms with that, and perhaps exercise more compassion and understanding in our interaction with these survivors.

Last but not least, the book brings to light other factors, namely; religion and family members in perpetuating domestic violence. While the writer is Muslim, the sentiments expressed in the book is applicable to people of all faiths and beliefs who use religion and culture as a tool of power to oppress and dominate. In a collectivistic culture like Malaysia, and most of Asia, it is very relatable to have an over-interfering family member who feeds into the abusive cycle, adding to the pain and trauma that survivors already feel.

Perpetrators abuse in various ways, and the deadliest of them all is the unseen psychological abuse that is done through deception, gas lighting, manipulation, and other means with the aid of family, culture, religion and other such tools at their disposal. This makes domestic violence an experience that is hard enough to explain, and let alone be documented for everyone to read. This book normalizes the experiences of survivors, their process of grief, their cycle of suffering and finally provides a possibility of building a new life free of violence – all from the point of view of a survivor. In Trust Overboard, Liya Red bares her heart and vulnerabilities in an attempt, that I pray, inspires hope in other survivors.

Puveshini Rao
EXCO Committee Member
Women's Aid Organisation 2017

ABOUT THE AUTHOR

Liya Red holds a Bachelor of Psychology with Honors, and Minor in Media Studies, from HELP University, Malaysia. She was the Vice-Secretary for Child Development Psychology (CDP) Club's trip to Johor, Malaysia, and Singapore, to learn from various psychology and psychiatry centres. She was a Facilitator for CDP Club, to visit the orphanage and the aboriginals in Genting Highlands, and a children's shelter home in Seremban, as part of Active Citizen Project. In Psychology of Film, the Dean's top choice was one that Liya directed, with the focus on child abuse awareness. She was also amongst top three winners in Educational Psychology for an educational game she created for children.

Liya received an Academic Achievement Award in Mont'Kiara International School, Malaysia, where she was under the International Baccalaureate program. She was amongst the first group under the Malaysian Studies Club to visit the less fortunate in Kedah, Malaysia, for the building of a school.

In Texas, Liya was honored with invitations to membership in the National Junior Honor Society (NJHS), as well as Family, Career, and Community Leaders of America (FCCLA). She was in cultural organizations such as Spanish Club, Asian American Club, and Klein Islamic Thought. She was in the Student Council, and also HOSA: Future Health Professionals. Liya was in the Design Team for Theatre Arts, and was the top student in her class for Interior Design. She won two gold medals for solo a cappella, representing Klein Independent School District. She committed to six months of weekends for Knowledge Exchange, accompanying elderly women at Barbara Bush Library, and committed to weekly visits, caring for Alzheimer's citizens at Atria Senior Living. She fed them, hosted

Bingo, and played the piano for them. Liya painted houses, and built houses, with Habitat for Humanity. She was also a trained Katrina Volunteer at George Brown Convention Centre.

Red has been professionally modeling since eighteen years old. She was a Fine Dining Front of House Hostess at Garibaldi Italian, and an Elite Consumer Engager for Philip Morris International. She has over twenty years of dancing experience with passion, ranging from ballet to pole dance.

Liya Red grew up in Houston, Texas, with her parents and four brothers. She is a middle child, and the only girl. She is currently residing in Selangor, Malaysia, where she got married into domestic abuse for three years, leading her to write a memoir.

This is Liya's first book. Visit her at www.LiyaRed.com for more information and updates.

www.ingramcontent.com/pod-product-compliance
Lightning Source LLC
Chambersburg PA
CBHW020338180726
47991CB00020B/1750

* 9 7 9 8 2 3 0 8 9 7 0 9 5 *